I Am My Cat's Bitch

I Am My Cat's Bitch

I Am My Cat's Bitch

By Lindsay N. Pendragon

I Am My Cat's Bitch

This book is dedicated to my brother

Stuart Frank Koons
1950 – 1967

With a special thank you to

Allison Collins

for sharing Josey the cat with me
when I needed a furry friend the most.

I Am My Cat's Bitch

Table of contents:

Table of contents (cont.):

Table of contents (cont.):

Disclaimer

I am not a veterinarian, a cat behavioral specialist, or cat psychologist or in any way degreed in cat anything. I am NOT an expert.

This book is for entertainment purposes only and should not be considered a guide or reference book for what you should do with your pets.

I am just a guy who has had cats around him almost his whole life, who has enjoyed their company for the most part, and who has a somewhat warped sense of humor about his relationships with the little beasties. This book is meant to be enjoyed, not analyzed or poured over for some great wisdom; leave that to the ancient Egyptians. (And my psychologist.) This is basically observations that I have made over the years and stories about cats that I have known.

This book contains opinions and observations made by me (and filtered thru the smoky glass of time); and most certainly not directions on how to treat your animal. The discussions between me and other people that I show in this book are as I can best remember after sometimes forty-odd years, so don't hold me to the exact wording. I may have accidentally mixed up people and places, again because so much time has elapsed in some cases.

Hopefully, this book will make you laugh, maybe make you cry, piss you off or make you think about how important a pet can be in your life.

You will have to excuse me as occasionally I will put on a professor's hat and give you some information.

I may say what I do about certain cat behavior and under certain conditions, **but always remember to consult a real professional if your cat (or any pet) is having problems, is injured or in distress.** What I do may not be what you should actually do.

Lindsay N. Pendragon

The author is donating 5% of his royalties from this book to various Humane Societies and Animal Shelters.

I am my cat's bitch.

Yes, it's true. With just one look, I am bowing and scraping before my feline overlord waiting to serve her every need. In that sense, I am my cat's "bitch." And as many of you out there can attest to, this happens all too easily.

One day you are happy in your lack of pet-tritude; the next day you own a cat.
Or a dog.
Or a ferret.
Or a rabbit.
Or a Komodo Dragon.
Or a (*insert type of animal here*)
But I think I know cats, (see disclaimer) so I'm sticking to just cats.

Sure there are just as many dog people out there as cat people; I see dogs out walking their People all the time. But I'm just going to talk about cats here; mostly about just two cats, Krysla and Josey. (And maybe a few other honorable mentions that I have owned or been associated with.)

Well, that's the other thing – you never *own* a cat. A cat adopts you, not the other way round. They should be referred to as People Adoption Centers for cats and dogs, or Human Centers instead of Humane Centers. Being called Animal Rescue Centers is probably appropriate; many a human animal's life has been saved, or lengthened, or made healthier by having been adopted by a cat or dog. (Not so much by a Komodo Dragon.)

Now, I'm a guy and guys are not known to be cat people. Hell, even gay guys seem to like tiny dogs over cats. (You just try dressing a cat in a cute outfit and stuffing it into a purse.) But I have always just preferred cats. It comes down to one basic thing for me. You ever notice how cats have a slightly clean smell, whereas dogs just *smell*? Besides, I'm basically lazy; I like a pet that can clean itself and doesn't need to be bathed.

Plus, I have a hard enough time worrying about picking up my own crap (figuratively) to be worrying about picking up a dog's crap (literally). To me, scooping a lump of *something* from a litter box (there's a surprise in every box!) is much preferable to bagging a steaming coil of what obviously just fell out of a dog. (No surprise there.)

And cats at least have some class. They prefer doing their business in private for the most part, whereas a dog is completely happy, delighted even, to take a dump anywhere. Both animals however lose points in the taking pees anywhere contest.

And then of course, there is the cleaning themselves up afterwards. This is an entirely different subject, and will have to be dealt with at another time.

So why do I consider myself my cat's "bitch"?

It all came about one day when I was feeding Josey and then standing with the door open waiting not so patiently for her to decide whether she was going to go out or not. A friend that I live with looked at me and said, "That cat's really made you her bitch, hasn't she?" Being a "bitch" in this case is like the prison slang for another inmate owning your ass. (Sometimes literally.) You just do what he tells you to do and your life is a little simpler.

Sigh.

And it made me realize, that yes, because I cared about Josey, and fed her, and cleaned up after her, and bought her toys, and made sure she got her flea medicine on time, and checked to see if she wanted in when it was storming outside, and waited patiently while she made up her mind about the million things that cats take their good old time deciding, I could probably be considered her "bitch".

But I get warmth. (When she decides to give it to me.)
And companionship. (When she decides to give it to me.)
And share in some humorous activities. (When she decides to do something other than sleep.)
And clean up the occasional "present" she leaves in the hall. (When I finally smell it.)
And pick up the hairball. (After I've stepped on it in my bare feet.).

All in all, I may just be getting the short end of this relationship.

Not really my cat.

Josey is not really my cat; she is Allison's. (But by now I think I could claim joint custody.)

I moved south from Ohio due to health problems and settled in with close friends and a cat named Josey. Josey was the cat of Allison, my friend's daughter. Allison was a Tween when she found Josey and she named her after Josey in the "Josey and the Pussycats" comics. (I wonder how many cats got that name the year those comics came out?). Then Allison went away to college, leaving Josey in a house full of dog people. Even with that disadvantage, she had managed to have them pretty well trained by the time I showed up.

The cat and I basically checked each other out for about a month. Josey had been a feral kitten when found and you know how long a feral cat takes to relax around anything new. (Forever and a day.)

At some point during that month, I started taking over the duties of feeding Josey. Originally, she would just walk through a room where I was, and glance my way once or twice. It was like being at a Sock Hop in the Junior High gym all over again. I'm not sure which of us was the wallflower.

Slowly, she worked her way up to sitting on the other end of the couch from me. Like bookends, or some old married couple, we would each do our own thing knowing the other one was there, but not interacting with each other. Then one day she sat right next to me. When I reached ever so slowly over to pet her, she flowed off the couch like liquid fur and was gone. Too much: too soon.

Time passed. She got used to me feeding her. I would talk to her like we were old buds, but she wasn't falling for it. That look on her face was one of "You are a food dispenser and a door opener; nothing more." She had been an outdoor cat more than an indoor cat when I came, so there was no litter box to clean. No way for our scents to intermingle. I wasn't going to use her litter box; just my handling it would get my scent on it. (Though peeing in it would have worked that much faster.)

I was watching TV one evening after dinner, when she approached. She stopped beside me as she usually did, gave me a few sniffs, then surprisingly; she put one paw on my thigh. I felt like a teenager on a date. (Okay, any guys reading this just barfed.) "*Anticipation*" as Carly Simon used to say. (Okay, you guys might as well just leave at this point.) It was sorta cool, sorta amazing all at the same time. Then, like it was nothing new, she walked up on me and lay down on my stomach. This was easier then; I was heavier and had a built-in couch for her to use. (Pregnant women know what I'm saying; that baby bump is easy to use for a plate holder, or a cat perch.)

She didn't stay long, but I could hear the ice breaking. Maybe she thought that I just might do. (In a pinch.)

I had been told to close my bedroom door at night, because Josey had left some surprise "gifts" in Allison's bed at different times. I had never had that problem with a cat, so I didn't worry. Besides, the mattress pad had a waterproof backing, so it would just be a matter of doing laundry if she did. And I did my own laundry.

Then one night I felt a thud as the mattress moved slightly. Padded feet walked hesitantly across my bed towards my face pulling on the bed sheet ever so slightly with each step. I turned my head slowly and looked at her. She was standing; ready to disappear at the first indication that something was wrong. Then she lay down about a foot away. Carefully, she slowly tucked each front paw under her chest. Almost closing her eyes completely, she watched me for a while. I fell asleep and when I awoke, she was gone.

Over the next couple weeks, Josey moved closer, and started sleeping for part of the night on a towel I had put on one corner of the bed. Everything started as usual one night, but at some point, she had moved up beside me, touching me. After that, we became friends. She will wait at the top of the stairs as I come up to go to bed. Then she'll run into my bedroom and sit on the bed where I can see her from the hall. She waits till I settle in, and then she joins me.

Maybe she's my cat now after all.

The cat who liked spaghetti.

Krysla.

She was an amazing cat.

Krysla was a short hair tortoise shell calico of medium build. Just a normal run of the mill cat to look at, but then you would pet her. Her fur was like mink. I had a girlfriend actually bring her mother's mink coat over so we could compare. You honestly couldn't tell the difference. Girls loved to pet and hold her. She would tolerate the attention only up to a point, and then she would make her adieus.

One night when I was leaving a girlfriend's apartment, I heard a tiny mewing. It was raining and I was going to have to ride home on my motorcycle. I just wanted to get going, but the mewing had gotten my attention. As I looked around the trash cans, I realized the sound was coming from inside one of the cans. Finally I found her inside a fast food bag. She was wet and covered with half eaten fries and ketchup. (I *really* hoped it was ketchup.) I knew my girlfriend was asleep, so I couldn't go back inside for her help. I figured the cat wouldn't get any worse in the short trip to my place, so I just put the bag with its kitten unhappy meal surprise in my jacket.

It mewed the whole way home.

At my house, I went into the kitchen and tore the bag open as I figured that would be the easiest way. There was this tiny little thing, wracked with shivers so bad it could barely stand. I took some paper towels and started wiping it off. It tried to get away but just didn't have the energy. Holding it in one hand to keep it warm, I got some milk out and warmed it in the microwave. I didn't have an eye dropper so I tore a piece of paper towel and twisted it into a point. Dipping the end of the towel in the milk, I then tried to get the kitten to suck on it. It wouldn't. The drops just ran down its chin. So I put the towel over its nose and mouth and when I took it away, the kitten licked its nose like I thought it would. Now when I offered it the milk twist, it licked it. Soon it was greedily reaching out for the twist before it even reached its mouth.

I laid a big twist full of milk in front of it which it licked away at while I started cleaning it again. Using a warm wet dish cloth, I wiped it to get the ketchup and gunk off of it. It would need a good washing, but that could wait. I noticed something in the fur around its neck. As I pulled on it, out came a maggot. I almost barfed. I threw the maggot it the disposal and with a quick br-r-r it was gone. From a long ago Boy Scout first aid lecture, I knew maggots only ate dead flesh. Still. Yuck. Looking at its neck, I saw a cut. I hoped it had come from a tin can and not by some twisted kid's hand. It wasn't bleeding. Still, it would have to go to the vet in the morning.

Having gotten tired of thinking of it as "*it*", I turned it around and lifted up its tail. It was a girl. Well, if she survived I would name her, but by then I needed sleep. And by its yawns, so did Miss Maggot. (Oh crap, that's definitely not going to be her name.) Now, every time I walked away from her, she would start mewing. That was going to make a long night. So I put on a plaid flannel pajama top that I keep around for the ladies that stayed over and put the kitten in the breast pocket. It was a good fit. It snuggled in and tried to wash its muzzle, but the poor thing was too tired.

Climbing into the water bed, I rolled onto my right side. The kitten was in the left pocket so she was okay. As I fell asleep, I felt a tiny vibration but no purring. I touched the kitten. It was her. That was my first surprise with this cat; she purred, but it was all vibration. No sound. She'd been alone long enough that she even kept her happiness secret.

I named her "Krysla" for crystal or jewel because she was a diamond in the rough when I found her.

There were many other surprises over the next eighteen years or so as I became familiar with this cat. For one, she played fetch. For another, she loved spaghetti.

I would give her table scraps every once in a while, usually flakes of fish. She wasn't a table cat where she would jump up and try to get stuff off your plate. (She did like to sit on my lap when I ate. Then she'd sneak a paw onto my plate when she thought I wasn't looking.) So I was surprised when I came back into the room and she was munching down on my spaghetti, noodles and all.

Every time after that, when I had spaghetti, she had to have her own little plate on the floor.

Garfield the cat and his influence on my life.

I started being interested in writing for a living about the same time that Garfield came out in the Sunday cartoon pages.

The early Seventies were crazy times. We had just come out of the Psychedelic Sixties, which I missed by graduating high school in 1969. Though I did have a Jimi Hendrix black light poster and I still have a clay pipe a girl made for me. It's of a bald headed man (think Jerry Garcia) with a hole in his head for the bowl. She said it was what I would probably look like when I was forty. (Forty was *ancient* to a twenty year old.) I was in college at an Akron University branch, but I was still working in a restaurant part-time to make enough money to go to college full time. (My parents were poor enough that we didn't have much for a "middle class" family, but we had too much for me to get any scholarships to go to college.)

That's when I saw my first Garfield comic in the Akron Beacon Journal. (The local paper didn't have a Sunday edition so people in my town either got the Beacon Journal or the Cleveland Plain Dealer.) Here was a fat slob of a character whose favorite food was lasagna. I was skinny at the time having had a long bout with mono in high school, but I loved lasagna. My mom's Italian food repertoire consisted of spaghetti with meat balls and lasagna; and the lasagna was a special occasion sort of dish.

Back to Garfield.

I didn't read his comic religiously, but if I got a paper, I would look for it. It was usually funny. He had a hopeless owner and was motivated by the simple – food is good. (Gordon Gekko ripped a version of this off from him in the Eighties.) It was something I could understand. I liked food. In fact, I would cook in quite a few restaurants over the next 20 - 25 years and work just about every position in a commercial kitchen. (Anthony Bourdain I am not, but I got around.) And thru all that time, when I got a paper, especially a Sunday paper, I looked Garfield up. Still do.

I even still have a small stuffed Garfield that I kept first on my typewriter, then on my word processor and finally on my computer until flat screens came out and he lost his perch. He is currently sitting on an old TV in my bedroom. Through thick and thin he has been there for me (at least his stuffed toy representation). He is probably the only constant thing in my life for the last forty years. (Okay, that's just sad; pathetic even, but still true.) Friends, seeing the stuffed Garfield, would give me Garfield cartoon anthologies for Christmas. (I also got the occasional *Doonesbury* collection.) I even watched one or two of the animated specials. (Lorenzo Music was the perfect voice for him.)

You see, Garfield was more than just a cartoon character or a stuffed toy. He represented a choice I made in my life to try to follow my dream and become a writer. In doing so, I moved out to California and tried to break into Hollywood as a writer. I counted it up once and I had put a million words on paper during my ten years in Ventura. I got close enough that I had an agent for a while, and got a couple meetings with producers and wrote a crap load of spec scripts. But nothing went anywhere. Then I wrote a novel and sent it to a bunch of agents and finally got one interested in me. The first novel she said would be hard to sell, but it showed that I could write, so I needed to write something more commercial. I started on a second novel.

Then the economy crashed and I lost work and had to move back to Ohio. This wasn't that bad because the agent was in New York. But I had received notice before I left California that I had Hepatitis C, which was considered fatal, back then. And I had to file bankruptcy because of the lost work. That was 20 years ago. I beat the Hep C, but lost track of my agent and basically stopped writing because I had to spend so much time making a living in a bad economy. Then, a year or so ago, I had to stop working again for another health reason. When I was packing up my stuff to move to North Carolina, I saw the Garfield toy on my computer desk. (I had even given my computer to my sister.)

And I thought that if I can't find work that I can do, maybe I can start writing again.

And here I am, writing again; because Garfield reminded me to try again.

Cats do the darndest things.

The four cold, wet paws in my armpit.

It's been a miserable night outside even for January in North Carolina. The cold rain has been off and on all night. I've been comfortably tucked away all warm and toasty in bed under my flannel sheets. (Plaid of course; I'm a Yankee and all flannel should be plaid.) Then, nature calls and I get up and go to the bathroom (or as a former girlfriend would call it, "The reading room"). I push the window up a few inches, as fresh air may be needed, and look for a magazine.

However, from outside there comes this mournful meow (with just a hint of whine that goes straight for the guilt nerve and makes it vibrate like a high C on a fiddle) and I make the mistake of spreading the slats of the blinds just enough to look out and see her. There she is. Wet fur matted down. Sitting on the deck hand rail out back, in a scene that just tugs at your heart strings and makes you silently go "ah-h-h'.

And in my case the "ah" quickly changes to "ah, shit!"

Now how the hell did she get out? She'd had her dinner and I had let her out the front door so she could fertilize the camellias there. (She prefers the front when the weather is bad because she can just two step it across the porch and down under the cover of the camellias.) And then I had let her back in about 15 minutes later when her business was done. Now she's back outside.

I don't mind leaving an animal out (especially one like her that likes it outside) when the weather is nice, or even borderline nice. Light rain in summer – is okay; thundersnow in February – not so okay. I am not a mean person.

I look back outside. It wasn't a mirage. She's still there. And I swear she lifted one paw up to her mouth and made a little cough; like some four year old trying to convince you that they're "really, really sick and need hot chocolate to feel better."

So, down the steps I go (and steps are a bitch for me due to injuries) and back to the dining room door off the kitchen. This leads out to the deck (and our poor little Camille). I look out before I open the door, because I know I'm going to get sprayed by the rain coming in around the door. No cat. Then I hear the soft "thud" against the door. It's the little furball throwing her weight against the door to get my attention. This cat is not subtle in any way.

As I open the outside door (and get rain splattered), Josey shoots past me (no hello, how are you or anything), hesitates to see if there's any food in her bowl that she might have forgotten from earlier (fat chance of that), and dashes out of the kitchen. I hear her rear claws clicking on the hall parquet like a flamenco dancer's taps, then silence. So she either went in the living room to clean herself up on the couch, or… She's on her way to my bed.

Damn. Damn. Damn. Damn. Damn. There is no way I will beat her up the stairs. She takes three steps at a time like Pavlova at the Bolshoi and I drag myself up one at a time like Quasimodo in the bell tower.

So by the time I get to my bedroom at the end of the upper hall, there she is on my bed licking the moisture from her fur. But she's not sitting on the towel she has as her blankey on the bottom corner of the bed. No-o-o. She is in the center of the warm toasty spot I had left when this madness all started what seemed like an hour ago.

As I push her aside with my butt (she doesn't deserve my hands), she leaves behind a damp cold spot for me. Thank you very much.

I snuggle back into the disarray left by my leaving and then her arrival, and try to get myself ready to fall sleep again. Straighten the covers just so, refluff the pillow and turn it over. I'm ready. I close my eyes and try to will myself back to sleep. Of course I can't. I'm wired now from all the trudging around, and down, and up and cold rain in my face. I'm never going to get back to sleep. Then the sheets start to stretch away from me and I know she's coming. And that means only one thing.

Yep. She comes up and pushes with her nose so I'll move my arm and then she snuggles up against me. AND PUTS THOSE DAMN COLD WET PAWS IN MY ARMPIT! All four of them; tucked in so that they'll get warm.

Now I'm pissed. I start to move away and she finishes with the *coup d'gras*. She puts her head on my shoulder and starts purring like her life depends on it (it does). And as I listen, and I want to push her away but my eyelids are getting heavy and I can't fight it anymore. I fall asleep.

And I know she has that little cat smile on her face as I do.

Tick. Tock. Her daily clock.

My cat's daily cycle.

Sleep.
Wake up.
Watch me sleeping. (I get a feeling when she's watching.)
Hunt (May alternate with prowling.)
Eat. Take a quick break. Yup, need to eat more.
Groom.
Outside.
Inside.
Socialize.
Repeat endlessly.

'Nuff said.

Okay. Really? Now you want to say hello?

You are sitting on the sofa, enjoying your morning coffee, maybe watching the news or the weather.

Your kitty wanders into the room. Eventually she makes a long snaky trail across the room, stopping to sniff everything along the way. She takes the time to rub a cheek against the important things, making sure that everyone knows that that item is hers. Finally, she ends up sitting beside you. You adjust your position a little so she will be comfy there. And as you look to see if she's okay, she sticks a rear leg out and starts cleaning the base of her tail. (Okay, you know what I mean.) You can only shake your head and go back to the news. Then, with little or no warning, your delightful furball stops her present action and decides it's time to come up and give you a morning hello. You get a wet furry mouth rubbing against your cheek moments after it was rubbing against her cheeks. (Again, you know where I mean.)

Just why have cats decided on that order of doing this?

Why can't they just say hello like a civilized being instead of visiting the funky fur first?

A friend (a dog owner) said that since the cat is looking at its a-hole, it is reminded of its owner and that causes it to suddenly want to say hello. I thought my friend was being a bit cruel about the cat's owner. (And biased, being a dog owner.) That conversation quickly went into a series of smart aleck remarks back and forth that didn't resolve the issue.

I understand that grooming has a high priority with cats. If their fur isn't kept neat and clean they can end up dying in bad weather. Grooming helps spread saliva and body oils that are beneficial to a cat. I also understand that part of their grooming and hygiene involves cleaning their backsides. I have also read some articles that suggest that cat saliva has certain mild anti-bacterial and deodorant qualities (one of the reasons why a healthy cat smells "clean"), but I'm not going to let my cat lick an open wound on me because of that. You should probably *never* let a cat or a dog lick an open wound on you. There are bacteria in their salivas that could be harmful to you. If Josey has been licking my hands for one reason or another, before I handle food or any communal item (silverware etc.), I wash my hands and/or use some sanitary gel. It's just common sense.

Now, anybody that knows me will tell you I'm not a clean freak. I stay clean and tidy, just not to an obsessive level. But it does bother me a little when one of my cats cleans itself and then wants to immediately say hello. All in all, I just don't think it's a great idea. I usually push Josey aside and scratch her head between the ears instead and she seems just as happy. (I'm sure she slips one past me every once in a while. That's part of being a pet owner.)

So, just when is the kitty kiss considered "clean"? It its strictest definition; it's never clean. Cats don't wash their paws except with their tongue so they are never really sanitary that way. Maybe if they just didn't wash their butts in front of us we could live in denial about where their raspy little tongues have been. As a pet owner, I vote for denial. (And that includes you dog people too. Don't you dare think this is just a cat issue.)

Again, I am not a doctor. If you have concerns about your cat giving you a morning kiss, talk to your vet.

I'm reminded of an episode of a sit-com where two roommates are arguing over using each other's stuff. One roommate reminded the other that they both use the same washcloth in the shower, and as he put it, "Just remember what I wash last and what you wash first with that cloth."

(Ew-w-w.)

It's hunting season.

All cats have a hunting instinct. (At least that's what I've been told.)

They may have not been shown how to kill their prey (Krysla wasn't; she just discovered it on her own), because either their momma cat didn't know or wasn't around to show them.

How a cat deals with this depends on whether your cat is an "indoor" cat, or an "outdoor" cat.

If she is an outdoor cat, then she is probably enjoying the real thing and hunting neighborhood squirrels, chipmunks, mice, rabbits and ground dwelling birds. You will probably know what she's hunting by any "trophies" she brings home. You will almost never see a domesticated cat hunting birds in trees. (*Sylvester* hunting *Tweety Bird* is a cartoon, and is not reflective of real life.) The closest cats will come to this is jumping at birds as they come down to birdbaths or feeders.

Now if your cat is an "indoor" cat, she will have some substitute behavior for the hunting requirement in her life. That is how the pet industry separates owners from millions, if not hundreds of millions, of their hard earned dollars. The pet owners (cat and dog, the pet industry is equal opportunity on this) are told they need various toys and devices for their cats to play with since they no longer have the real stimulation of actually hunting.

So you are shown aisle after aisle of cat "toys" which you are told are really "hunting substitutes" for your cat. You are also told that it is very important for your cat to satisfy these "hunting" urges. Your cat will spend hours happily playing with its new toy. (Yeah, we'll see about that.) Some of you are saying "My cat loves his springy-thingy." I'm sure some cats do. And some cats also fall over backwards when they clean themselves.

I have seen a lot of these toys in the bottoms of closets and on garage sale tables in the driveways on weekends. I don't know if the salesman had been very persuasive about them, or the cat got bored with them quickly. Either way, that $29.95 toy is now a $1 special in Joe and Marge's driveway.

I was told when I moved here that Josey would not play with such toys. Krysla wasn't into toys either. Tigger liked his ball in the ring, and some toys that hung on springs and elastic bands and bounced when he grabbed hold of them. So I've seen cats have a take it or leave attitude towards toys.

However, Josey has come to like the "scratchy noise under the blanket" game; or as I prefer to call it, the "Quit biting my toe!" game.

It goes like this. My sheets are 300 thread counts, and for some reason that seems to be the perfect thread count to get a nice "scratchy" noise when I quickly move my finger nails back and forth on them. Prior to this discovery, I couldn't get Josey to fall for things like moving your hand or foot under the sheet to get her attention. Krysla loved the foot chasing game and I probably have a couple scars on my foot to prove it.

Well, I will make the scratchy noise under the top sheet (And most recently under a blanket too. Her teeth are like needles.), and Josey's ears will perk up. She raises her head like a submariner's periscope to get a better angle on this new situation. Her eyes move back and forth until she sights the moving finger or toe. There's a tightening of the shoulder muscles, and WE'RE OFF! (Watson, the game is afoot!)

As a variation, I will make the scratchy noise under a pillow. For this, Josey dives forward with her paws and legs outstretched in front of her like a plow, driving herself forward with her back legs. She usually ends this version of the game by bulldozing the pillow the whole length of the bed and off the end. With a soft thud, she ends up on top of the pillow. The game resumes after a quick time out for a little grooming. Then she rushes up from the bed's end and attacks wherever the sheet is moving.

The total game may only last ten or fifteen minutes, but at the end of it, Josey is happy. She sits there, cleaning her paws and muzzle like she just nailed a gazelle on the Serengeti.

My cat uses me as a salt lick.

Occasionally I will break down and actually do some physical work. Not often, just occasionally. Lately it's been the vegetable garden I started and I'm rearranging the flower beds.

Afterwards, as I sit on the back deck admiring my work and enjoying a cold one, Josey will come by to say hello. When she gets up close, her whole demeanor changes from bored kitty to ravenous wild cat that wants to eat me. Well, actually she wants to lick the salt off my forearms and hands.

I would think that with all the additives and things that are put into commercial cat foods, (there goes my endorsement fees) Josey would have no problem getting all the salt she could possibly want. But no, it seems she still needs some directly from my skin. And she doesn't just take a couple quick licks and find me distasteful like most people do. Nope. She wants to make a meal of it. She starts licking away like there is no tomorrow. Long slurps with that raspy shark skin tongue of hers. I put up with the pain knowing that I will save a fortune on exfoliation treatments later. (Now if I could just get her to do my face.)

You do realize that a cat's tongue is raspy like that because wild cats use their tongue to lick the last bit of meat scraps from the bones of their prey. So Josey now thinks I'm a gazelle. (Okay, something slower and fatter; a soft skinned hippo, with a limp.) Now at some point this little exercise of hers in remedial feeding starts to become painful. I think I can see where she has removed all the tanned skin and is starting to work on the sub dermal layers. I gently pry my nice domestic kitty (Who is growling at me as I do this.) away from my arm and set her on the chair beside me.

I guess she's not done because she jumps right back and starts licking faster this time. She's either trying to get enough licks in before I can remove her again, or she thinks I'm going to melt in the sun. I mean, she is really going at it. She has wrapped her two front legs around my forearm to hold on. Again, I pull her off my arm and getting her with both hands, I gently toss her away from me. (A gentle two handed kiddy toss, not a Hail Mary with three seconds to play in the final quarter.)

She starts to come back and I stand up.

This is getting both ridiculous and worrisome. (I am reminded of the dream where I die alone at home and she doesn't know how to use the can opener.) You can now imagine a fairly large, somewhat muscular man hurrying away from a nine pound cat that just wants to lick him. It looks like something out of a *Benny Hill* episode on BBC. I make it safely inside the house and close the screen door tightly behind me. Josey stands up on her hind legs with her paws on the screen.

This sounds ridiculous, and it is; but it is also true.

Now she's licking her paws.

I need to look up cat nutritional supplements on the computer. Or get a tranquilizer gun.

Little blue eyes. (They're just so damn cute.)

Ol' blue eyes was the singer Frank Sinatra.

Little blue eyes are kittens. Most seem to have that gorgeous sapphire eye color that clothes designers would kill to be able to reproduce in a fabric. And then there are the erect little tails. Kittens are the dune buggies of the animal kingdom.

If you have ever watched a group of kittens running around on the blankets and sheets on a disheveled bed, their short tails constantly stick erect like the whip antennas on dune buggies. They charge down the slope of a folded sheet and race back up the blanket on the other side in their frenzied chase of the rest of their litter. From their eye level what they can probably only see all the time is their stubby tails racing to and fro. It's like in the desert with dune buggies; their whip antennae with flags on the end to tell other drivers where they are as they zip to and fro behind the dunes.

My first experience with a mass kitten invasion was when Krysla had her first litter. She had made a nest and had the kittens. Seven or eight of all different hair length, color and breed. (Cats can have kittens from multiple fathers in the same litter.) Other than checking on them daily and changing the nesting material (old underwear I had kept for dusting) every couple days with clean ones, I hadn't thought about them that much. Krysla seemed ok in her maternal duties, and the kitties never got very far from a nipple.

Then one morning, after I had gone to the bathroom and looked in to check on Krysla and her brood, I had returned to bed for a sleep in. I was about half awake; my head lay on the pillow, when I saw the first tail. *Jaws* had just come out that summer and as I saw the tail cruise by behind a tossed aside blanket, I could hear that theme song in my head. *Da dum.* Then another different colored tail came from another direction. *Da dum.* Then suddenly, more tails had arrived. (Captain. We're going to need a bigger bed.)

I sat bolt upright. Between lack of sleep and a hangover from the night before, this was getting too weird. Then I saw a kitten crawling his way up and over the edge of the bed. Scaling the coverlet like some mountaineer going up the north face of Everest, its tiny claws making the perfect crampons for scaling the linen cloth. Oh, crap. Their tiny claws were snagging on the linen. (It was an expensive gift and I didn't want to have to explain the damage.)

As I reached for Sir Hilary, all the other little beasties were running amok on the bed. You ever try to herd cats? Don't. It's impossible. Finally, Krysla jumped up on the bed, landing among the mewing and mayhem. Only to walk over to her pillow, high stepping over her own children on the way, while giving me a look of "Oh, you have them under control, I see." and flop down on her pillow.

Now, I've heard enough of my friends describe the "delights" of child rearing to understand that Krysla was probably worn out by the birthing and raising of the kitties. She looked disheveled and she wasn't groomed as well as was normal. But she wasn't sticking me with these little monsters. Yes, they had gone from "how cute" to "little monsters" in about two weeks. Little did I know what was in store for me over the next month.

They climbed *everything!* Anything that they could sink their little claws into, they climbed; or at least tried to climb. If they couldn't climb it, they made sure you knew they had tried by the frayed fabric or shredded everything else.

Slowly, their stubby little tails lengthened and their little blue eyes turned green. And the spell was over. The gorgeous blue eyes were nature's way of making sure you didn't throw them out with the wash water. But once the blueness was gone, you could think clearly again, and you knew it was time to thin the herd. Anyone that came to the door was asked if they wanted a "darling" kitty. I almost convinced two Jehovah's Witnesses that I would only take their literature if they took a kitten.

It was hard work, but I finally got rid of the last kitten. Then I took Krysla to the vet to make sure neither of us went through this again. Only to find out that Krysla was pregnant again!

Coming soon, "Little blue eyes" the sequel – "*Revenge of the kittens.*"

Out of Africa. Big cats, little cats — not the same.

I hear people say, "My little tabby is descended from lions and tigers." (And bears. Oh, my.) "That's why my cutikins is so ferocious." And then they take their declawed cat's paw in their hand and make a swiping motion at you with it while the cat is dying of embarrassment.

Not true. They come from two similar but different evolutionary tracks. (I was curious enough about this to look it up.)

Yes, they may have had a common ancestor 35 million years ago, but only if you really want to nit-pick it. Lions, tigers, jaguars and leopards are of the Pantherinae subset of the Felidae species of cats. Whereas, domestic cats are of the Felinae subset: along with cougars, cheetahs, lynxes, ocelot and the wildcat. Though it had been thought that domestic cats came from an ancestor out of Africa, it has been recently discovered thru genetic testing, that the domestic cat is specifically descended from the Near Eastern Wildcat that roamed thru the Near Eastern (Turkey to Egypt) section of the Mediterranean.

About 8 – 12,000 years ago, when humans were switching from hunter/gatherers to farmer/herders (and attracting vermin to all their stored grain), the wildcat saw an easy living and began the domestication of man. Really? You ask incredulously. You are honestly going to sit there and tell me that man domesticated the cat? Yes, at night, Mr. Farmer/Herder would close the windows and lock the door to keep Domestic Kitty 1.0 in the hut. Well, we all remember how successful *Fred Flintstone* was in putting his cat out for the night, so obviously there should be no problem for Mr. 10,000 BC in keeping one in. Now, let me think about that. Oh, yeah. There were no windows or doors in those crudely made mud and stone huts. There were just holes in the outside walls where doors and windows would eventually be.

No, the cat domesticated man to fulfill the cat's need for food and shelter. Cats are smart. When the cat domesticated man, it was in the cat's best interest so that man would keep the tabby safe from all its predators.

The domestic cat followed humans as they spread out all over the world. They began to diversify (there are actually 37 different species of all cats, big and little, in the world today), and fill niches wherever they could. In Egypt, they were worshipped. They could be seen on ships, in temples and castles, and traveled along the Silk Road to China and the Far East. They were *everywhere.* And still are.

It is estimated there are 600 million domestic cats of all breeds in the world today.

People forget when they go to zoos and safari parks that that big sleepy tiger out there sure looks like Tabby's older brother (on huge amounts of steroids), but he isn't. People die because of errors in judgment like that.

In my mind, when a person tries to keep a big exotic cat like a tiger in a domestic situation, he is just asking for an accident to happen. Even if you get that tiger as a tiny kitten, it is still a wild animal with all its instincts (such as the one to hunt and kill) still in place. You have no idea of when those instincts will overcome all the training and love you have given that animal.

When I was in college, there was a guy down the street from me that had a pet lion one summer. He knew some circus people some how (I never heard the whole story) and that's how he got the lion for the summer. Though it was just a cub, it easily outweighed a large Lab and was slightly bigger in size. This guy kept the lion in his front enclosed porch and thought it hilarious when someone would come up and knock on the door and this lion cub would answer by standing on its hind legs with its paws on the door frame. I damn near wet myself when it happened to me.

This guy was pretty irresponsible in my mind. Initially he never even strengthened the door lock on a flimsy screen door; but after the cub had broken out a couple times and wandered around the neighborhood, he reinforced the door. I heard that the local police finally enforced a law to get the lion returned to its proper owners (that and the cost of feeding a large cat; they don't eat crunchies). This just underscores my concerns when people try to "adopt" big cats of any type. Some of these people can be fully trained professionals working to rehabilitate animals that had been kept under cruel conditions, and some may just be big hearted people with good intentions that want to have "exotic parks" for kids to experience wild animals up close, and others may just keep the animals as captive targets for would be "big games hunters". I really think the best place for wild animals is in the wild, or a professional zoo.

You may want to pet the big, pretty kitty, but that big, pretty kitty wants to eat you.

What's so great about a "crinkly" noise?

You've all seen your cat do it.

She will purposefully find the paper bag that "crunches" a little better than the other bags or the plastic store bag that has a "crinkly" sound. (Store bags are slightly stiff; plastic grocery bags are mercifully soft.) If she could pop bubble packaging sheets with her (non-existent) thumbs, she would.

What draws a normally stealthy creature to make as much noise as it can?

Your cat discovers one of these noise makers (usually at 2AM). All you want to do is sleep, and all she wants to do is show you how cool this new noise is. ("Look Food dispenser animal", she says. *Crunch ... crunch ... crunch.* "Isn't this neat?") She even drags it into your room so you can appreciate it better. You've got a meeting in the morning with a new client, your husband has a diesel truck revving its engine in his sinuses and you desperately just want some sleep before the kid comes in to announce some new tragedy that has befallen Dolly during the night.

So you get up. You find whatever the cat has found, pat the cat on the head like "nice kitty" (when you really want to strangle it) and stuff the noisemaker down as far as you can in the first wastebasket you see. With a tired and only slightly satisfied smile on your face, you return to bed. Just as your eyes are closing for the last time tonight, you hear "crunch... crunch ... crunch, crunch, *crunch.*" You turn on your back, look at the ceiling and slap both hands flat on the sheets in exasperation.

Kitty has found another noise maker.

Now, it's either try to hold the pillow against your head all night, or look for those ear plugs you bought last time your dear husband said he didn't snore, or try to catch the cat and put her outside. You sit up on the edge of the bed. Shuffling your feet around, you can't find your slippers so you give up trying. Meanwhile, your cat has been watching all of this and now takes off with her party favor. You stop. Maybe she has given up with it for tonight. Nope. She just moved a little farther away but not so far that you can't hear it. Finally, after several attempts to catch her, the cat has run into the family room. You decide it's far enough away that it won't disturb you and you close the door behind her. Muttering to yourself, you make it back to bed and fall asleep again.

During the week as you find the time, you gather all the possible noise makers up and either tuck them away for future use or trash them. Eventually, you are distracted by other things and forget to finish the job. You don't think about it again until next time.

But why is your cat, (and mine a*nd* your neighbor's) attracted to making noise in the first place? This is an animal that prides itself on its stealth. This is an animal whose life literally depends on being able to be quiet while it does things. So why is it trying to be a one man band?

I honestly can't figure it out, except that it just wants to have a little fun. Like a two year old that has discovered banging pans with a spoon, your cat just likes the noise.

Now, it just needs to work on its timing.

The classic standoff. (High noon at the screen door.)

Your cat has finished its dinner. It's grooming its muzzle and whiskers.

You are finishing up the dishes and want nothing more than to go into the living room, kick your shoes off and watch something on TV, or finish that book you've been reading. You see your cat head for the back door. As usual, as soon as she eats, she wants to take a stroll. She's at the back door slowly pacing back and forth. You're wiping your hands on the dish towel as you go to let her out. You open the screen door. Suddenly, as she nears the door, she just sits down.

No matter what the real time is, you've reached that time I call "High noon at the screen door." It's the classic, "Are you going out or not?" stand-off. I can hear the whistled theme from "*The Good, the Bad and the Ugly*" start in my head. Then a clock starts ticking, getting ever louder as you wait. You're getting tired of holding the door. The cat starts cleaning its paw.

Simple, you say, screw holding the door open; get a cat flap put in the outside door. Unfortunately, in our neighborhood that flap door is an invitation for all sorts of varmints to come in, rather than for kitty to go out. You really don't want to come home and find a raccoon making a Dagwood sandwich from the contents of the kitchen wastebasket. Meanwhile, your cat is either on top of the refrigerator all fluffed up, or sitting outside on the window ledge, looking in and having a good laugh.

Then get a litter box, you say. Let kitty do her business inside. Well, it's not just about kitty's digestive tract.

I find that even an indoor cat needs to get outside, have a stroll and check out the neighborhood. It needs to do *cat* stuff. It needs the stimulation of watching birds, chasing squirrels, having stare downs with other cats and tormenting as many dogs as it can. It should have a real breeze blow thru its fur instead of the exhaust from the air conditioning vent. Even if your cat just goes out on the front steps, it's outside, and that's good for it.

Back at the stand off, you decide the cat can wait, so you close the door. At this, your cat dances around and then runs thru the house to the front door. You follow. (Well, that's the way to the living room anyway, you tell yourself in your mind.)

At the front door, there she is, just waiting for you with a smile on her face. As you get closer, she starts her little soft shoe dance again. (Left paw over the right, right paw over the left, and spin, then again.) Then as you open the front door, she freezes. Leaning forward in that weird way like a chameleon moving along a branch, she sniffs the air a couple times. She might even do that thing where she opens her mouth a little and breathes in deeply. (She's actually using additional odor sensors in the roof of her mouth.)

Nope. She hisses and turns away from the door. She smells something she just doesn't like (a tom may have come along and marked your door). Whatever the reason, she's not going out *that* door.

Now, at this point, she may run thru the house to the back door again, and go right out without any fuss, or just go into the living room with you. Whichever, for me, it's "I've given you your choices. You chose neither, so I'm watching my show now." She may stay quiet for just a few minutes, and then start the whole thing over again. Or she may quiet down and watch your show with you for a while. Some nights, Josey will go thru the whole thing three or four times, before she finally goes out. (Or I pick her up and put her out. I *know* she needs to go out to pee if nothing else.)

I hate to forcefully put her out. (I don't toss her out like a football. I just pick her up and set her outside the door.) I think that ejecting her brings up some memories for her. Memories that trouble her, because she will be standoffish when she first comes back in, then she's clingy the rest of the night. She's all lovey-dovey and won't let me out of her sight. I'm not a cat shrink, but that seems to be the action of someone that has abandonment issues.

Josey doesn't give me the "High noon" experience every day, just often enough to be a pain. She *is* choosey about which door (we do have a tom in the neighborhood that chases her) depending on what she smells. Krysla was never choosey; if she wanted out, any door would do. (If she *really* wanted out, a screened window would do.)

I also think Josey is nervous about going out due to her feral youth. I've noticed that she will take a mouthful of food (if any is available) before she goes out. It's like she is worried that that bit of crunchies might be her last mouthful for a while.

She shouldn't worry; I am her bitch after all. Besides, no cat, or any pet, (or human) should ever have to feel that way.

They make special cleaners for this, I think.

Is that *smell* in the hallway something I should worry about?

You know the smell, the one with the ammonia scent. Yes, your kitty has had an accident. Though I don't think the word "accident" is appropriate since the little beastie knew exactly what it was doing at the time.

I had one cat, Rhianna, a beautiful ginger longhaired tiger that just didn't understand what a litter box was for. She peed everywhere; on the hall carpet, on the dining room oak flooring, on the kitchen tiles and on the bathroom linoleum. Everywhere except in her damn litter box. It was a period when I had three cats; Krysla, the mom, and Smoker and Rhianna, her two kids.

Smoker, a short haired gray, had his own issues that I will discuss separately.

Both of the kids were about a year old and I had just been busy and hadn't found homes for them yet. Krysla never shared litter boxes. Whenever she had kittens, the little guys used one box (all seemingly wanting to pile into it at one time, flicking litter on each other and the floor in the process, then dancing around outside the box and shaking their paws to try to get every last granule off) and Krysla had her own. Since Smoker and Rhianna were siblings and had grown up sharing a box, I figured they would be okay continuing to share. Wrong. Maybe it was because Smoker was a boy and Rhianna a girl that they required separate facilities. Whatever the reason, I ended up having three litter boxes in my house for a while. I don't think they made multi cat litter formulas back then. (This is 40 years ago.)

Krysla's litter box had always been in my bathroom on the second floor. I put both the kid's boxes in the half bath on the first floor that was rarely used. That didn't seem to work out. That's when Rhianna started having accidents. Interestingly, she never peed on any of the furniture, or the beds (my water bed or the queen in the spare bedroom), just on the floors. This was when I discovered that companies made special cleaners that they proclaimed would remove the cat urine smell from the peed upon article. These worked to various degrees, but never seemed to get rid of the entire after odor. I even put baking soda in their litter boxes to help neutralize the ammonia. That didn't work out well either.

I had had both cats fixed at the appropriate time, so I didn't think there was any issue with their plumbing. Finally, I just called the vet. (Poor guy, I seemed to bother him incessantly.) After I explained everything, he said I seemed to have done everything that he would normally suggest. The last thing was for me to bring Rhianna in to have her checked out. ($40. My own doctor only charged $25 for an office visit back then.) The vet found nothing wrong and could only suggest that I separate the kid's litter boxes, which I did when I got her home. There was a balcony sunroom on the second floor at the back of the house and I put Rhianna's box there.

Still didn't help.

Not too long after, a friend of the girl I was seeing stopped by. She ooh'd and aw'd over Rhianna and about a month later took the feline off my hands. I had warned her about the problem and she said she didn't have any other pets. And blessedly, Rhianna settled in at her new home and the peeing stopped.

Looking back now, I think part of the problem might have been that I just didn't have enough time to spend with all three cats. Rhianna's bladder problem might have just been a cry for attention. In her new home, she got plenty of attention and so she didn't need to cry out for it. Cats are social animals; they need time with others, and not just other cats. So if you plan on having multiple kitties, you had better plan on spending some time every day with each one.

Just think- a few minutes of affection could have saved me from having to sand and refinish some oak flooring.

Not as disgusting as it sounds. (But close.)

Cats are territorial. That's a simple fact. But how that wrangling for territory is expressed makes all the difference.

My friend's cat, Valentine's Day (V.D. for short) did not take kindly to strangers. When a new kitten came into the household, she reacted by basically trying to kill it. The only thing that saved the little furball (other than my interference) was the fact that V.D. had never been shown how to kill by her mother. She would get the kitten in a stranglehold, but didn't know how to finish with the coup de grâce.

Many cats will "mark" their territory by rubbing the scent glands in their cheeks and paws against the object in question, or say an entry door. ("*Cat*", the character in the British futuristic sci-fi series "*Red Dwarf*" had a different way of marking his territory.) This is why when your kitty is rubbing up against you with her body as she waits impatiently for you to get her breakfast, she is just saying "hello"; but when she rubs her whiskers, and therefore her cheeks, against your leg or her bowl or an object like a table leg near her bowl, she is actually marking all of them (you included) as "hers".

However, I have to say that my cat Krysla had the most unusual way of marking her territory and showing just who the top female was.

Krysla and I shared a Victorian house not far from the college campus in my Ohio hometown. When I was college age and dating, if I was lucky a girl would stay over for the night. I had a king size heated water bed which had its benefits in convincing the young lady to stay rather than go out into the cold winter's night. The walk of shame was better done after breakfast and while a warm sun was glowing in the sky.

Nothing happened for the first couple of times that I had visitors. Then one night, I had gone to the bathroom. As I was doing my business, I happened to look at the litter box which (I thought appropriately) shared the bathroom and saw something sticking out of the litter. It looked like the elastic band on a pair of underwear. I went over and gingerly pulled what I could now clearly see was panties, out of the clumped clay grains. I was certain these were the bikini panties belonging to the girl asleep in my bed. I was in deep doo-doo (just like the panties had been) if the girl saw them this way. Given the confusion of the moment, I wrapped them in a face towel and threw them in the laundry basket.

The next morning, after a futile search, they couldn't be found. I suggested that the girl leave and when I found them, I would drop them off at her dorm room. She wasn't happy about it, (I guessed that a walk of shame without panties was just a little colder in the winter) but she agreed. After she left, I threw them in with my laundry and ran them thru the wash. Delivering a now clean pair of panties later that day, I explained that I don't know how, but they had ended up in my laundry. ("They must have been on the floor under stuff that I gathered up to wash" was my lame suggestion.)

Unfortunately, this became a pattern. And a problem.

I could cover a one night stand, but when I had a repeat guest it was impossible to use my standard excuse more than once. (Plus, girls talk among themselves, and I was beginning to get a reputation I didn't want.) Frantic for a way of fixing this, and suspecting Krysla was involved in some way, I called the vet. He laughed when I had explained. He said that he hadn't seen such an extreme example before, but Krysla had decided that no female scent was going to be stronger than hers: female pheromones were female pheromones whether it was cat or human. Therefore, to cover my date's scent, she had buried it under her own. The vet suggested I was lucky Krysla hadn't decided just to pee over *all* the girl's clothing.

So, from then on, I tried to make sure I kept track of my date's underwear (that reached humorous extremes at times), *and* made sure Krysla was locked in the kitchen where she had food (and a back-up litter box) when I had overnight guests. Still, this strategy was not successful every time. (Passing out and dealing with all this *and* a hangover too in the morning was not my idea of fun.)

It surprised me that Krysla didn't do her new trick when it was just a quick stop and go with a friend during the day. But it only happened when it was an overnight experience.

Still, I guess I should have just been happy for small favors.

These are two (three?) of her favorite things.

Like humans, and all other animals that can taste things and enjoy those tastes; I think cats must have their favorite foods.

And like most things that we really enjoy, they are probably bad for us, and the cat.

Josey loves cream cheese and ice cream fingers.

Oh, and cheese puffs end caps.

Sure there's the occasional almost empty tuna can that she will push around the kitchen floor (Like a hockey player with the puck.) with her nose stuck inside until you swear she's eating the can itself. But just try and take that can away before she's done. You will hear this weird low growl that sounds something like Grandpa trying to shift gears on the tractor crossed with a pig's grunt and you know to back away, until she walks away. Now, you can't tell me that's not one of her favorite things.

I'm sure that everyone out there that shares a room with a cat can easily describe something (or many somethings) that their cat loves to eat. Are they good for your cat? Who knows? Do we mean nutritionally good: or just yummy good? Again, who knows? For everyone that loves to eat a certain item, there are probably just as many people that hate it. Certain societies eat insects. You won't find one on my plate except by accident.

As a chef I heard the sayings, "People eat the sizzle as much as the steak itself.", and "People eat with their eyes." This means that we associate not only the taste of something, but the sound (in this case) and the look with the finished product. We eat the whole enchilada.

It makes me think. Josey likes to stare at the moon. Would she like to eat the moon? The moon was supposed to be made of green cheese after all. Would your cat enjoy a piece of Swiss that has obviously been in the back of the fridge so long that it has become a scientific experiment? If the moon is green cheese, then Mars must be quesadilla dip. All orangey reddish colored with craters from the bubbles that oozed to the surface thru the viscous liquid and popped?

Now, let's get back to Josey's favorite things. These are just three examples of foods I know she loves. How do I know? Somehow, without being in the same room with me, she knows I'm eating these things. I'm sure the crackle of the bag gives the cheese puffs away. But how the hell does she know I'm getting cream cheese out of the fridge, or ice cream out of the freezer? Is it the sound of the doors being closed? She doesn't come running when I'm getting some fruit out of the bin, just the stuff she likes.

Then, her specialties have to be served a special way too. Both the cream cheese and the ice cream need to be served via the end of my index finger. I think she likes chasing the food as it melts and runs around my fingertip like the spinning teacups at the county fair. You know, having a meal with a show. Then for the cheese puffs end caps. I have to bite these off, making sure I only get the ones that are extra orangey. Then I hold it for her to sniff (like the sommelier holds the cork for the wine bottle), when she nods, I drop it to the floor where it is quickly dispatched.

I know it is probably the salt and the fats that attract her to these foods. And let's be honest, just like they attract me. (And you too.) And they are undoubtedly bad for her. (I only give these to her as treats, not every day.) In fact, I'm sure I will hear from vets and pet owners alike about how horrible it is to feed a cat these things. (Look in your own fridges and cupboards, hypocrites.) But at least I'm not an idiot that sits there feeding their *Fifi* chocolate bonbons. I make sure there are no philodendrons or Easter lilies in the house that can actually kill the little furball.

So maybe we all need a few treats once in a while: just not a steady diet of treats. Besides, they wouldn't be special if you had them all the time.

My favorite college ice breaker.

I was still a bit shy in college. (Believe it or not, I was.) I wasn't athletic and I was a bit of a nerd. (Black glasses and pocket protector type of nerd.) One of my brothers had died my sophomore year in high school in a motorcycle accident and that caused me to withdraw even more.

The college in my hometown was an expensive private school with a lot of East Coast kids whose daddies were company CEOs, doctors, lawyers, actors, etc. and/or came from old money. I mean, some of these kid's families had *buildings* named after them. One girl's family had a *city* named after them. Some of the students were of the third and fourth generation having gone to this school. I was from a lower middle class family and my father sold vacuum cleaners. Never the twain shall meet was my thought. But I became involved in the family business and expanded it into stereos, TVs and records (when we started, we sold 8-track tapes and 45s), and that started to draw a lot of college student business my way. I had already started hanging out in the Student Union to play pinball (I loved "8 ball") and eat at the college snack bar. I went to a state college but did homework at the snack bar. Thus I had entered their orbit and become just one more student among the masses.

So I started dating girls from the local college. But being shy and a bit goofy looking, I needed an ice breaker.

Enter *Pepe LePew*.

If you grew up watching Saturday morning cartoons you are probably familiar with Pepe. He was a French skunk that sounded like Maurice Chevalier. He was infatuated with a hapless cat that accidentally got a stripe of white paint down her back so that now she looked like a skunk. Star crossed lovers if there ever were any. So Pepe was forever chasing this kitty/skunk. She was frantic to avoid him. He was ever so coolly following her.

My connection to all of this was that when Pepe finally catches his object of desire, he did this ridiculous "Le purr, le purr, le meow-ow-ow" accompanied by his head being rubbed against her shoulder. This may sound incredibly stupid, but if I was in a conversation with a young lady at a party, and it was sort of going my way. (Liquor helped.) I would suddenly do this "le purr" thing that Pepe did (including the head rub).

You would think I would get slapped, or the girl would look at me like I was insane and run away. That happened, but only about 10% of the time. The other 90% I would get a funny look, then the girl would laugh and sometimes pet my head like I was a cat. Sometimes things you would never guess would work, actually worked.

I was happy as a cat loving skunk when it did.

The cat as an alarm clock.

Josey has several wake-up modes. Unfortunately she doesn't have a reset or a snooze button.

The "courteous wake-up" is when she reaches out and gently, even daintily, taps my shoulder with one paw, and even waits for my reply before nuzzling up against my shoulder. She will adjust herself like a demure lady making sure there will be no problem with her dress as she sits. She places her two front paws on my shoulder. Then she slowly "walks" herself closer with that little rocking back and forth as moving forward thing cats (and snipers) do; purring contentedly as she waits like a Geisha about to serve my tea. Sometimes she will continue after a few moments. Moving across my shoulder, she steps into my armpit, does an about-face and lies down with her head on the inside of my shoulder this time. I will scratch her head between the ears and begin our morning conversation.

"Are you hungry?" She looks at me like I'm an idiot.
"Of course you are, or you wouldn't be bothering me." She blinks at this which is her version of "Duh."
"Give me a minute and we'll go downstairs." She's on her own schedule and leaves to go downstairs now.

This is the most preferable of all her wake-up modes.

Then there is the "Why must you stand on my chest?" mode. As it implies, Josey walks up on my chest and stands there looking at me. For some reason she thinks this will motivate me to get up and feed her. What it does do is motivate me to roll sideways so she has no chest to stand on.

However, she has learned a new version of this. After I roll her off, she climbs back up and lies down on the side of my abdomen which is now my top side. The cat is persistent.

Next is the "Why did you jump on the bed and hit me in the nuts?" mode.

I don't think it's intentional, but she has amazing accuracy. She's like a three year old with a Whiffle ball bat. She will charge into the room at full speed. I've been warned by the thundering sound of her paws on the stair steps. (Amazing how loud a cat on carpet can be when it doesn't care about stealth.)

There's the soundless leap and I'm sitting bolt upright with my eyes watering. Like a furry gymnast, she knows how to stick her landing.

It's a tossup between the last two as which is the worst, but I'll go with the "Race back and forth across me to get my attention" mode.

This one is basically what it sounds like. Again, the thundering race makes its way up the steps, followed by the leap. But as I turn my groin away from the door in anticipation, she misses and lands just past me. Now, like a bull that has missed the matador, she turns and charges; running right across my ass to the floor. Here she turns again and paws at the floor. In rapid succession, one paw after the other fully extended out, then back, then the other, then repeat. It's a really bad workout video or the smallest, fluffiest bull you've ever seen. Then she runs right across me again, turns and runs back across me and out the door. (Sometimes I can hear her go all the way down the steps before she stops.)

This one always gets me up because of the pawing bit. Krysla used to do that to tell me she needed to go to the littler box, but I hadn't cleaned it yet and she would rather go outside. Sometimes I will go downstairs and Josey will be beside the door dancing like a two year old that has to go. Or other times, she is patiently waiting by her bowl for morning crunchies (at 4AM? I don't think so). At this point I will go back up to bed and close the door.

If she stands outside the door mewing, the bowl thing was a feint and she really does have to go outside.

Finally, there's the "Why did you just give me a Wet Willie with your cold wet nose?" mode.

A Wet Willie, for those of you that didn't have a childhood, is when someone licks their index finger, sneaks up from behind and sticks the wet finger in your ear (or both ears with both fingers if he's a pro). Josey's version is to sneak up, pull her whiskers back against her face so they won't touch me and announce her presence, and then thrust her cold, wet nose into my ear while purring as loudly as possible.

This gets me every time. It's just unnerving. Plus that cold wet nose bests a warm wet finger every time.

When you find a tiny, little trophy on the pillow beside you.

It's like a white trash version of a scene from "*The Godfather*"; you wake up and there's an animal's head in your bed.

Only in this case it's not a horse's head, but some little varmint's noggin.

Your cat has left you a "trophy".

I've heard several possible reasons for this action:
1) Your cat is making a comment about her meals not being fresh enough.
2) Your cat confused "Get in bed." with "Get me a head."
3) Your cat has seen "*The Godfather*" way too many times.
4) Cats will bring you trophies to show you their prowess in hunting.

Yes, it's number four. (Though Josey has seen *The Godfather* a couple of times.)

Usually they won't go so far as to bring it into your bed (Krysla did), but they will bring different body parts and leave them for you to see.

I've never seen this behavior in indoor cats, probably because they just don't get outside very much. (Hence the name "indoor cat".) I would have to say that a cat that is totally content on being inside has no real killer instinct. The most vicious thing it has ever dealt with was probably a dust bunny.

Krysla was really the first cat I was around that shrank skulls for me to see.

It started with a couple tails (from mice I guessed), that appeared on my front mat. They were a bit of juxtaposition to the "welcome" on the mat. I kicked them aside with the tip of my shoe not thinking that they meant anything. Then one day, I came home and there were four or five heads of chipmunks on the mat. The weird part (and I swear to God on this), the heads were arranged in descending order of size. That sort of freaked me out a bit. I thought I might need to watch the neighborhood kids to see if any one of them might be harboring bad thoughts (against me or the world).

This continued off and on during the summer. When I found one of the heads on Krysla's pillow on the water bed, I decided it had gone too far. I also realized it wasn't the kids; it was my cat. A couple weeks later, I had to take Krysla to the vet. While the vet was examining Krysla, he asked me if she had any problems or weird behavior. I knew he meant sneezing or biting at her fur and stuff like that, but I mentioned the chipmunk heads. I said that at first I thought it might be the neighborhood kids having a demented laugh at my expense.

The vet said, "Nope. Your kitty here is showing you that she's a good provider." He explained that cats would bring home trophies to show off their hunting prowess. He asked if she ever was around when I discovered these "surprises". I said occasionally she was. He told me that next time she was present when I found more trophies; I should pat her affectionately and tell her "Good kitty." I looked at him like he was a little strange, but decided it couldn't hurt.

So next time that I came home and there were trophies on the mat and Krysla was there, I petted her head and said, "Well done." or something equally odd. I let her in and while she watched, I gathered up the two corpses in a napkin I had in my pocket. I slipped them into a fast food bag that I had brought from the car to throw away. Later, while she munched away on her dinner, I disposed of the bodies in the trash which I then took outside. I really didn't want them in the house.

This happened a couple more times and I increased my show of affection each time hoping that she would get the message. Finally, she must have figured it out (or just got bored with it) and the trophy displays stopped.

I was glad it had stopped. It had creeped me out a bit.

The alfresco nosh.

Most cats are content with their bowl of crunchies with little soft pâté of something spread on top (like caviar on toast points; I keep telling you cats have class) And a small bowl of water (with a tiny carafe beside it).

Some just like hunting squirrels.
Or chipmunks.
Or mice.
While others specialize in birds. (My Mom absolutely hated it when Princess would kill a Robin.)

Hunting is part of their daily cycle. But most cats just substitute chasing a feather on a string or a ball in a ring, or playing with your baby's mobile in the crib, or even a laser pointer's red dot (be very careful not to shine it in their eyes). The hunting instinct remains in even the most domesticated tabby and it needs to be satisfied; so (though I know I have derided them elsewhere) thank goodness for the cat toys. (Just don't overdo it.)

But regardless of how many civilized distractions, some cats still feel the urge to kill. I read somewhere that cats are the largest predator of small birds in the US and Britain. You try to suppress the urge to hunt in cats and you end up paying for a cat psychologist who gives you a prescription for cat anti-depressants (you ever try to give a cat a pill? Wear heavy gloves). Or worse yet, for a guru who tries to adjust her aura to a better color.

I think there are three categories of hunting behavior:
1. Hunt and release.
2. Hunt and eat.
3. Trophy collecting (and maybe a little nosh).

"Hunt and release" is when a cat chases down a squirrel (we had tons of squirrels in my hometown) and then maybe plays a little with it, and finally gets bored and walks away. (The squirrel has either fainted or is playing dead at this point.) The cat playing with its "kill" is usually because it doesn't know how to kill its prey. Part of the Momma Cat's schooling of her kittens is teaching them how to actually kill the animal. Remember in one of the *Jurassic Park* movies where the Momma T-Rex drags a guy home to its babies, then lets them kill the guy? Sorta like that but on a smaller scale. (Maybe it would help the world if a cat had a big game hunter or a lawyer snack once in a while.) The cat is not tormenting the squirrel for fun; it just doesn't know what to do at that point.

Krysla brought a chipmunk home one day while I was on my porch. She sat there with one paw pinning the animal to the sidewalk looking at me with that "what do I do now?" look. I sure as hell wasn't going to snap the little thing's neck for her. (It would be like killing something out of a Disney cartoon.) But in the process of trying to get it away from her, I heard a little "crunch" when she bit it, and it stopped moving. I went to get a bag to put the corpse in to throw away, but it wasn't necessary. While I was gone she had made the connection between the "crunch" and food (perhaps it reminded her of her crunchies) and all that was left was a tail and the head.

"Hunt and eat" is just what it says. Your cat has a wild side that is just under the surface and it will come out occasionally. Maybe it just needs "the real thing" once in a while instead of crunchies and pâté. As a football player I knew used to say, "Meat good."

"Trophy collecting" is just what it sounds like. Your cat has gone out and killed something: then brought the little corpse (or part of it) back to show you its prowess at killing. (This is the cat version of going on safari.)

Whatever the reason, your cat will sometimes resort to its wilder ancestry and go out for a fresh nosh.

The cat's "raspberry".

Is it a malfunction of her tongue; or a statement about your relationship?

I think most people know what a "raspberry" is. But for those unfortunate souls that don't; it is when someone sticks their tongue partway out and expels air over it making a "phu-u-t" sound. Or in a cartoon, the tongue would be huge and stick all the way out and wiggle as it is "phu-u-ting" amid massive amounts of spit.

You've probably seen a cat sitting somewhere and she has this contented look on her face. But her tongue is stuck halfway out, like she has bit down on her tongue and hasn't realized it yet; or like she is giving you a raspberry without the sound.

What does this mean?

Is this the feline version of the universal one fingered hand gesture?

Or is she so content and relaxed she didn't have the energy to pull her tongue back in all the way. Perhaps it's a new feline yoga movement. (The Sphinx doing a raspberry stance.)

I think we should blame it on the ancient Egyptians.

Somewhere, in some temple (maybe Luxor, maybe not), tucked away in some dusty corner near a hieroglyphic advertisement for hemorrhoids and lower back pain for tomb diggers; there's a drawing of a cat giving a raspberry to a priest. And she's doing it to his face. (Cats were viewed as gods, so they could get away with anything.)

If a dog did this; it would look stupid (stupider?) If your mate does this (without the sound), check for a stroke.

I think it's just one of those quirky things that make a cat, a cat. People have quirks, why can't cats? (This is just a universal quirk instead of a personal one.)

The magic bowl (And you're the genie.)

The food bowl, or as Josey probably thinks of it – *the magic bowl*.

It's magic because it always seems to refill itself when she's not around. (Well, sometimes when she's there, but she's so blinded by hunger that she doesn't notice me as she shoves me out of her way.) It always has something good in it (at least by her standards). Occasionally, she even gets a treat. Regardless, I make sure she has her two square meals a day.

Josey's magic bowl seems to have a direct connection to her bag of crunchies and the tins of pâté. She is the first cat I've had, or at least been in charge of, that doesn't seem to like table scraps.

That surprises me, because as I've said, she possibly started out as a feral kitten. Plus, cats just don't seem to refuse food. *Any* food. I understand that some cats are turned off by various spices we humans use on our food, preferring their meals au naturel et alfresco. But if a cat is hungry enough, I see it eating anything. (Well, except maybe something that is spicy hot.)

I was dicing up some leftover turkey the other day to use in a casserole, and I put about a nickel sized piece of white meat on Josey's dinner tray. (That's not what it sounds like. Her bowls are on an old circular serving tray to make clean up easier.) She just sniffed it and looked up at me. Then she sniffed it again, and used her paw to push it off onto the floor. That was subtle. Then I thought, maybe she just likes dark meat. So I gave her about the same size piece of leg. Nope. That was onto the floor after one sniff. Now Krysla would have downed both with one bite like a Great White after a surfer. Not Josey; it seems her tastes have been refined.

Krysla too went thru what I called her snooty phase.

Suddenly, she would turn her nose up like the Queen at a Beggar's Ball at anything she didn't desire at the moment. And that damned moment kept changing all the time. I would feed her this brand of grilled mixed whatever. She would snarf down the first can with glee. So the next time I was at the Food Bunny, I would stock up on that brand. Come dinner time I would open up a can. Krysla would come over, sniff it and start a loud vocalization in how it didn't suit her tastes now. Since my Cat-Speak is somewhat imperfect, we went thru a month of - like it, don't like it. I was starting to wonder what the hell I was going to do with all the extra cans of rejected food. (The local food pantry ended up taking them. I didn't realize that they took in unopened pet food for the needy's cats and dogs too.)

Finally, Krysla decided that she wanted her original crunchies. How did I know?

Simple, she had pried open the cupboard door (there was a butter knife there beside the door, but I really don't think that she had used it), and had gutted the bag of crunchies like a trout on the fishmonger's counter. (We have to keep Josey's crunchies in an old coffee can with a snap on lid for the same reason.) The center of the bag had been torn open and the tiny multi-shaped food biscuits were everywhere. She lay beside the bag with her front paws on the crunchies like she was guarding her kill from the hyenas. She would take the occasional nibble just to taunt me as I watched. Finally, she was sated. Have you ever seen a cat burp? I did that night. Normally she wipes her muzzle with her paws when she is done, but this time, if she had had shirt sleeves, she would have wiped her whiskers on those instead (ask any man, it's just *easier* that way), just to mock me further.

The magic bowl is always there, always waiting in the wings for its command performance. Sometimes its understudy table scraps make an appearance, but Josey always comes back to the star. She knows the magic bowl will always come thru for her; will always delight her taste buds.

However, it may be a magic bowl, but the genie's work is never done.

Kitty dreams.

Your cat is beside you.

You're reading a book and Miss Kitty is sleeping off a big meal of pâté smeared over crunchies with a side of a special treat. This is just a typical after meal exercise in human/cat interrelations. Then, all of a sudden, your cat is running in place. It seems like she is trying to qualify for the Olympics in her sleep. (This could be an interesting event: sleep running. Well, there *is* sleep walking.) She's making noises too. Just what the hell is going on?

Your cat is having a dream.

She finally hit the REM stage and she's running after some prey, or running from something. No way to really know what's going on in that furry little head. Krysla had dreams. Bubba Kitty had dreams. Josey has dreams. It's just part of that wonderful experience of a cat being a cat. I understand that dogs also have them. What other members of the fauna of Earth have them, I don't know and don't really care. This book is about cats, dammit. Those other critters need to get their own writers.

From my experience, cat dreams fall into three groups:
1.   Running in place.
2.   Lip smacking good dream.
3.   Hissy fits.

"Running in place" is just what it sounds like. Your cat is running but not going anywhere. Like in humans when we dream, your cat's brain switches off most of the cat's nervous system while it's sleeping. But it leaves just enough motor control to allow the cat some form of expression of the event. (It also allows the cat's warning system to be on in case something nasty comes towards kitty.)

The "running" I've seen cat's do is actually similar to the way *"Pepe LePew"* runs in the cartoons. If you've seen these classics, Pepe leaps (excuse me, floats languidly) up in the air, then just the tips of all four paws move like he's paddling a boat, then he lands. Up, paddle one stroke, land. When Josey runs in her sleep, it's the same thing: just the ends of the paws move. Only quickly in a sprint compared to Pepe's lethargic motion. I wish I knew when she is about to do this, it would be great to ease up against those paws and get rid of that itch I can't reach.

A "lip smacking good dream" is when cats make noises when they sleep. Josey has several noises that she tends to repeat.

1. She makes a rumbling in her throat; not a growl, just a really deep purr.

2. She talks with a "Meow, mew, meow, meow, merowl, mew" sort of kitty speak; like she's having a conversation with another cat. It's very quiet. They must be in an expensive restaurant: *Les Gordo Chat*.

3. And finally (my personal favorite), she smacks her lips. It …is …hilarious. It's almost too quiet to hear, just "smack, smack, smack." Almost like the sound a baby makes in the high chair when they discover strained prunes are actually better than they sound. If I catch her doing it, it's hard not laugh out loud.

I am guessing that "hissy fits" are not expressions of something lip smacking good. More "bare your teeth and let whatever it is know you're ready for a rumble."

All the cats I have been around would do this.

They are sleeping quietly, then suddenly it's "Hiss! Hiss! Spit. Hiss!" and they jerk awake and shake their head. I think the human equivalent is you're dreaming about falling and your arm drops over the edge of the bed, and you wake up holding onto the ceiling fan. In feral cats, they may be reliving some traumatic event from earlier in their life, before they had you to take care of them.

Whatever, it doesn't seem like the cat has just had a pleasant experience.

All I know is when Josey has one of these "hissy" dreams; she will get up, shake it off and resettle against me.

And she always cuddles in a little closer than she was before the dream

That über contented look.

My sister sent me a birthday card one year that had this little gray/white tiger kitty sitting on the hood of a Mercedes car with that perfectly contented look a cat can have. What I call the "über" contented look.

Now, that particular photo may have been altered slightly to enhance the contentedness of the kitten, but you have all seen a cat give some version of the look. A look that says – all is right with the world and I am its supreme leader. I am the Top Cat, the Big Cheese (well, that's actually the mice version of it), El Supremo. You get my point.

But what exactly is the cat content with?
  1) Life in general?
  2) One specific thing about its life?
  3) The quality of its last meal?
  4) The bliss of the moment?

I think we have a winner; the bliss of the moment.

Like most non-human animals, the domestic cat is concerned with food, shelter, a sex life. You know- the important things. But I think the domestic cat takes it one step further. It has an ability to find bliss.

And what exactly is bliss?

It is that perfect moment (and a moment may last longer than a few seconds), where the cat is truly content with what it has at that moment. Everything has just fallen into place and gelled into something just so cool, so wonderful, that you just give in to the moment. You just live in that moment for as long as it lasts. No more, no less. You can't force it into existence, but you can easily destroy it.

A cat's face was designed to show that moment.

So, the next time you see that look on a cat's face, close your eyes, and maybe, just maybe you might be able to catch a little bliss yourself.

The difference between cat and dog owners.

To me it boils down to the fact that dog owners want something they can control, whereas cat owners want a companion.

I know that just pissed people off, but that's the way I see it.

Yes, dog owners want companionship too, but it's mainly about the control. That's why dog owners get so mad when their dogs don't obey them. That's why they feel the need to train their dogs to do something, and then show what the dogs can do to their buddies. "Heel, Rover!" and the dog obeys its master.

Cat owners? Hell, we know that little furball is not going to obey us unless it just happens to be what they want to do too. Say "heel!" to cat and if it could flip you off, it would.

I'm not saying that dogs aren't great pets- for some people. Just not for me.

Dogs need to be washed; cats don't. (In fact, just try washing most cats.)
Dogs want constant attention; cats could care less most of the time.
Dogs come up and butt their noses in my crotch and smell my ass; cats tend to stay away from both.
Dogs need their waste cleaned up all the time; cat's poo can be taken care of on your schedule, not the cat's.
Dogs are sloppy eaters; cats are dainty eaters. (Though I did have one cat that tore into its food like a Great White.)

Cats aren't perfect either.

Cats have attitudes sometimes. (OK, all the time, but sometimes it's a good attitude.)
Cats lick their asses then want to lick your face. (I try to make sure the cat eats something in between. Not that that really helps.)
Cats get pissed off quickly about seemingly nothing. (But usually want to cuddle soon after.)

Cats and dogs introduced early on in a family are usually there to teach the kids about how to be responsible. (Parents choose something else for this. This is a horrible way to teach responsibility. It almost always fails.)

Cats and dogs introduced later on in a family are usually kid replacements for Empty Nesters.

Cats and dogs just appeal to different types of people. Yes, we all know some couple that has both. But upon investigation, you will usually find that one adult had a dog before they met, and the other had a cat.

Then there are those people that have cats, dogs, fish, birds, snakes and hamsters all at the same time. People! Each kid does NOT have to have their own special pet. Have a *family* pet. There will be less chaos and your house will smell a hellava lot better.

And yes, visitors to your house can smell all the pets when you open your door to greet them no matter how clean you think you have made your house. You really don't want them to think they are visiting the elephant house at the Cleveland Zoo when they come over for dinner do you?

Moderation and responsibility. Just like drinking; too many and you're out of control.

So, each to your own and don't impose on people that don't like pets. If you have friends coming over that just don't know how to relate to pets (not just yours, but anyone's pets), then have your cats and dogs spend the evening outside or in another room. One evening of separation from your pets won't endanger your relationship with your animals, but it could strain a friendship. So be courteous and consider your friend's needs too.

(Scratching them behind an ear probably is not a good idea.)

Talking to the animals.

I really dislike when people talk to animals in "baby talk". This mostly seems to happen if the person is an overly made up older woman, an airhead heiress or an actor.

People! The animal can't understand what you are saying! No matter how you do it, cats and dogs will not understand the human language, especially if you say it in that cutesy, wutsey way people do in these situations. Hell, I don't think even babies like baby talk. We are not Dr. Doolittle.

And I don't like calling "Here, kitty-kitty." to get their attention. It's like going out and calling, "Son. Son." to get your kid's attention. I know it's just alliteration and it's probably no different than me going out and doing my "kiss- kiss" noise to attract Josey's notice, but it just irritates me. The cat doesn't know the difference. It's just an arbitrary noise that the cat will associate with a particular action.

A lot of people just call out their cat's name, which is okay in most cases. I have to bring up one case where it wasn't okay. My friends in Ohio had a cat called Valentine's Day, because that was when they got it. Their kids however liked to call it by its initials. And frankly, I hated standing on the front porch and yelling, "Here V.D."; especially since we were just across the street from the college's student health center.

As I said, I have always just made certain noises that the cat eventually attaches to whatever I am doing when I make that certain noise. An air kiss is usually what I do to get their attention. (Hey, it works for me.) Or occasionally, I will "meow" instead. Once I have their attention, I will say "Meat" if it's time to eat. And the little beastie will usually come running. If they are dancing around like a two-year-old holding his crotch, I will say "Out?" and usually Josey will run for the door.

So I have found that the simplest one word statements or questions (not commands; a cat doesn't do commands) are usually the best. The cat is recognizing your voice first, then associating the word with an action that you have repeated enough times for it to have made the connection.

Then of course there are the times when you just go stupid and start having whole conversations with your pet. (I'm home all day as you might have guessed.) This does not mean you are crazy, though people might think you are. Just don't talk to the animal all day. Then you do have a problem.

Go out.
Volunteer.
Make friends.
See a shrink as a last resort.

A pet is a good companion. Just don't make it your only one.

.

The Zen of laying in a sunbeam.

What could be more Zen than laying in a sunbeam?

It's snowing outside. The wind is howling and rattling the windows. The fireplace isn't giving off much heat. But find a good strong sunbeam coming through a window, and lay in it. The dust motes in its rays seem like fairy dust drifting down and giving you contentment.

Watch a cat laying in a sunbeam. You could swear it has a little smirk on its face.
Just pure bliss.
Lying there.
In the moment.
And nothing else matters.

Try it yourself next time your cat has put their mental beach towel down on the Navajo White beach of your carpet. You don't have to go for the fetal position Josey likes, or the all stretched out sprawl that Krysla preferred. If you're into yoga, try a lotus position.

I think cats are more the practitioners of Tai Chi. If you have ever watched them stretch out after a good nap; you can see what I mean. Oh, yeah. Head down low, butt up in the air, stre-e-e-tch way out and I'm doing "the plow" now. (Huh, I guess that's yoga after all.) Well, when they stretch out one leg and move it sideways, that's sorta Tai Chi.

Who do you think the monks learned it from? The Yeti?

Well, regardless of their Asian exercise motions, just watch a cat in a sunbeam. You will have to do this quickly because the cat will *sense* (the third eye is always open) you soon enough. She will open one eye (just partway) and give you that "Watcha lookin' at? *You lookin' at me?*" eyeful. Then disdainfully, she will write you off as nothing important and no threat, and go back to her bliss.

So, I say just find your own sunbeam (she will not share hers) and find your position, and slip into that wonderful bliss of the non-moment.

Om-m-m, kitty. Om-m-m.

Indoor or outdoor cat?

This would seem pretty straight forward; an "indoor" cat is always indoors, and an "outdoors" cat is always out.

Not so simple, Grasshopper.

I would consider Josey an indoor cat, but it turns out that before me, she was mostly an outdoor cat. Now, she is indoors most of the day sleeping on my bed, and only wants out at night when *I* am asleep in my bed (naturally).

Most days, she gets me up and we breakfast together. While I watch some morning news, she wanders off or if she's feeling needy, she will sleep beside me on the sofa. Then I go back to bed and she joins me about 10AM for her morning rubdown/armpit nap. I usually get back up at noon to start my day.

She finally gets up about 2PM and after trying to talk someone into giving her a snack, will go outside to take care of number one and two. (She has no litter box and goes commando with a tiny roll of toilet paper. She is a girl after all.) If it's a really nice day, she will stay outside for a little while. (I think she is checking out what's available on the alfresco menu.) Then she comes back in, and if I'm available, she gets her afternoon rubdown/armpit nap. If I'm not available, she will pester anyone that's around to try to get an early dinner. (If successful, she will still try to convince me later that she failed just to try to get an extra meal.)

So, I would say that Josey is inside 70% - 80% of the day, and outside for bathroom and socializing breaks. That would make her an "inside" cat. But the weather is getting warmer and I don't like being awoken at 2AM to let her out, so she will start going outside after dinner and come back inside when I get up for breakfast (unless she makes a nuisance of herself, whining around the kitchen door until someone lets her in). Now, that would make her about 55% out and 45% in. Not quite either an outdoor or indoor cat.

See what I mean?

Then there were my sister's cats: Sneakers and Mr. Stubbs (aka Stubby.) These two were strictly indoor cats, having virtually no interest in the outside world other than (*squirrel!*) what they could see from her windows. She has a second floor apartment with plenty of trees, so they have a good visual life. If they had been campers, they would have been found in the luxury RV and not in the pup tent. (Well, they would probably never be found in a *pup* tent.) Still, if these two spent 10% of their day outside, it would have surprised me.

When I was young, a lot of kids I knew had cats (and dogs). I didn't really keep track of their coming and going, but I would say that mostly they were like Josey and Krysla, more an inside cat in the winter and an outdoor cat in the summer. The only real outdoor cats I saw were the farm kid's cats. They were definitely outdoor cats. Some never came indoors for anything I was told; most staying in the barns with the other animals.

So, indoor or outdoor?

I think it has become a revolving door these days.

I want MORE now!

At some point after moving in with my friends in North Carolina, I took over the duties of feeding Josey, their cat.

Josey's diet is basically the same as most cats in America; some crunchies, a little meat pâté (the mashed up stuff in a can) and a bowl of water. There is nothing special. We rotate the canned stuff between four different products so she isn't bored. (I am, but she doesn't seem to be.) I measure her food out so she gets the right amount, but not so much that she turns into the Kitty that Ate Cleveland. She doesn't get any table scraps.

All was going okay, until I noticed Josey had started carrying more junk in her trunk than usual. She had developed a definite bulge that made her look like a cross between a tabby and a python that had just eaten a goat.

I thought, well, it is the middle of the holiday season and we all are putting on some weight. But I decided that Josey had been overdoing it somehow. Like I said, I measure everything, so I don't know where she was getting the extra calories. Regardless, Josey needed to go on a diet.

After some research, I found that most cat food makers had some sort of "reduced calorie" food. I got a small bag and started introducing it into Josey's meals. It was a crunchy, so I just substituted the new stuff for some of her old stuff. She seemed okay with the new blend, so I slowly started increasing the ratio of new to old. She should be getting less calories overall.

At some point, I went past Josey's desire to tolerate the new reduced diet. I had fed her and was standing near her bowl talking to my housemate. As I started to walk away from Josey, there was this "Hiss!" and I felt two paws trying to grab my pant leg. I looked down and moved my leg away and there was a repeat performance of "Hiss!" grab, grab, grab. It was a little pathetic because Josey has no front claws, so when she tried to keep me from getting away all she did was slap my pant cuff back and forth. Then, it struck me what this was all about.

Josey wanted more food! I had to laugh. Josey was bitch slapping my pant leg to tell me she just wasn't going to take it anymore. She wanted MORE and she wanted it NOW.

Just to see if I was right, I gave her a few more crunchies. Not many, just a half dozen or so. But that calmed her right down.

She snarfed down the bonus crunchies, then walked away giving me the tail straight up salute (Which I believe is the feline version of the human one finger salute.) Once she got around the corner, she stopped to groom herself. But when I walked into the hallway, she stood up and it was the straight tail salute all over again. She was definitely sending me a message.

However, when it came to bedtime; she jumped up on the bed with me, gave me a look of "You know I had to do that earlier, that was about *food,* but it's bedtime now and I just want to snuggle in and get warm like usual."

Josey has never held a grudge with me (so far), but she has told me a couple times since with repeat performances, that she wanted MORE.

I still laugh every time when she does it.

Hey, I remember you.

I think cats need to get reacquainted with their owners every day.

About 4AM, I feel the sheets moving as her steps get closer. She will walk up and sniff the left side of my face. Then she will jump over me and sniff that side of my face. And then another jump back to the left side again. She waits; she reaches out with one paw and touches my shoulder. I give a quiet "kiss, kiss, meow" and only then she will walk across into my armpit and curl up there.

We have begun our morning ritual. Half asleep, I rub her head between her ears, and after a few minutes, her head slowly droops down to my shoulder and she closes her eyes purring happily to herself. The purring becomes intermittent, and then stops. She's asleep. Then I fall back asleep.

Now it's 5:30 in the morning and I'm up. Even though I'm not working a nine to five job any more, I still get up early from twenty years of habit. As I sit there upon my throne thinking of what I should try to get done that day, I see a shadow enter the bathroom. It hesitates, and then jumps up on the lavatory. Slowly, it walks my way, stopping to sniff at anything interesting (which is everything), and finally coming to a stop beside me. Her head moves closer, and I move my head a little towards her, and then I feel her whiskers touch my face.

Finally, after a bit of sniffing, Josey rubs her cheek against mine, does a little minuet on the lavatory and rubs the other cheek against me. That's it. We are officially reintroduced to each other and marked as family.

This happens every morning come rain or shine.

I haven't been able to figure out why she doesn't rub my face to mark me as family when she first approaches to get her morning head rub and armpit nap (after sleeping eight hours, she needs a nap). Sometimes that head rub will last a half hour or more, but she waits until later. I would think it would be more important to accept me as family before letting her guard down. (Ok, you're family. Now I can have that nap.)

After all, we have just spent the night together. Well, usually. Sometimes she gets huffy and decides to sleep under the dresser. (If that is supposed to be a punishment for me to be left in the big soft bed while she sleeps on the hard floor, well so be it.) My bed smells like me (except for her spots), so what's the big deal about re-establishing a relationship?

I think it might go back to the litter.

You're piled in a jumble with your kin. But all the smells are new (you know the strongest smell belongs to the Big Momma Milk Factory that you are sleeping against). So every morning, once you have learned how to groom yourself somewhat, you start sorting out who's who in the fur pile. The easiest way to know who you have already sniffed out is to mark them with your own scent. So you bump against another furball. Yep. Smells like Fred with an overlay of me. And you move on to the next furball. It's a little easier once you can open your eyes. Now you can match the smell to the face. (Dogs match smell to the butt; a system that obviously needs some work.)

So, every morning Josey and I go thru the "Hey, I remember you." routine. Not too bad, all things considered.

(I am so glad that butts are not involved.)

(Sigh.)

Bubba Kitty. (The cat with two names.)

Yes, Bubba Kitty is the cat with two names. His other name is Nightmare. Why? Because I called him Bubba Kitty; but after I moved out, he was renamed Nightmare by my best friend Jim. I continued to call him Bubba Kitty.

Bubba Kitty (B.K.) had a strange life. (He was put to sleep in 2011 at age 16 due to old age.)

B.K. was originally Marie's (Jim's step-daughter) kitten. Not too long after Marie got him, she was in this horrible car accident and has been disabled since. B.K. came to stay with us (Jim, Jim's wife Inez and myself) after the accident along with Marie's two year old son. I was living with Jim and Inez after I had moved back from California to my hometown in Ohio. At that time, Jim and Inez had another cat called Valentine's Day (for when the kids got her) which was shortened to V.D. Confused yet?

Bubba Kitty was just this little long haired black furball with huge paws. I told Jim he was going to be a big "Bubba" of a cat by the looks of those paws. And I was right; he turned into a big Bubba of a cat. But as a kitten, he was terrorized by V.D. who chased him endlessly. She was queen of the house and wanted no one else in her realm. She was extremely territorial. So was Krysla, but with Krysla it came out in a different way. I think V.D. would have killed Bubba Kitty if she could have caught him. But she couldn't. Why? The little bugger was *fast*; he came down the stairs three at a time. And he always ran straight to me for sanctuary. He would leap towards me from about ten feet away and burrow into my shirt to hide. This was funny when he was tiny; but would just about cave my chest in when he weighed fifteen pounds (like having a bowling ball tossed at you).

When B.K. first arrived at the house, I was the one that played with him most of the time. I had missed having a cat since Krysla had died (at Jim's house) while I was in California. Bubba Kitty was filling that role for me. He was soon sleeping in my bed for safety. He would hide out from V.D. during the day. As he grew up into full fletched Bubbadom, V.D. stopped with the torments. He was bigger than her by then. He would hear my voice in the evening when I came home, and then he would stroll into the room and want his head rubbed.

Then Bubba Kitty started tearing all his fur out in big clumps. He would just rip them out. He was starting to look horrible and was turning into a mass of scars and leaving bloody spots on the furniture. Finally, the vet figured out that he was allergic to flea bites. We gave him some meds and he quickly returned to normal. I had thought that all the episodes with V.D. had stressed him out and he had developed a nervous condition. So I was glad when he returned to his "just a big furball" lifestyle.

I'm putting on my teaching hat now. This whole thing has a couple lessons:

1) You need to watch for abnormal behavior in your cat. It can have many different causes.
2) Territorial issues will sometimes crop up between cats. Introduce a new cat slowly into the household.

When I was finally able to move out on my own, I had to leave Bubba Kitty behind. He wasn't really my cat, even though whenever I would visit, he would be in my arms in a matter of minutes after my arrival. It was after I left that Jim renamed him "Nightmare". Well, Jim had always called him Nightmare. And I had always called him Bubba Kitty. It's amazing that the poor furball didn't develop a split personality.

I missed not having him around, but it wasn't meant to be. We were just passing thru each other's lives.

Cat names.

It would be so much simpler if cats could just tell us what their names are, rather than us trying to come up with one for them.

These are just a few of the cats that have crossed my path. I'm sure there are others that I have forgotten.

Sneakers. Socks. Mittens. Bootsey.
Krysla. Crystal. Jewel. Princess.
Bubba Kitty (aka Nightmare). Blackie. Blackbeard the Cat.
Smoker. Gandalf the Grey.
Brownie. Ginger.
Tiger. Tigger. Sgt. Stripes.
Marshmallow. Fluffy. Furball.
Josey.
Rhianna.
Mr. Stubbs (aka Stubby).
Leo.
Princess.
Valentines Day (aka V.D.)
Bell. Belle.
Pywhakit.
George. Georgina (after George had kittens.)
Owl.
Captain Jack. Whiskey.
Katmandu.
Daisy. Dizzy.

People give cats names for all sorts of different reasons:
        Because of whom they remind them of.
        Because of their color.
        Because of their markings.
        Silly reasons.
        Named after a favorite character on TV.
        Because they were drunk (or stoned) at the time.

I just wish people would put more thought into it, or at least ask the cat if she/he likes it before making it permanent. How would you like to be stuck with a name you didn't like all your life?

Where not to put the litter box.

Oh where, oh where does the litter box go?
Oh, where, oh where does it go?
With its sides filled high and its clumps not dry.
Oh where, oh where does it go?

Any place other than the dining room would be my first guess.

Finding a suitable place for a litter box can be a pain. When Krysla was with me, we lived in a large house; an old "painted lady" as Victorians had once been called due to their elaborate paint jobs. The bathroom was quite large (about 12 x 15 feet) so there was plenty of room. Besides, it made sense to me that her litter box was in the same room as mine. It also made sense because I usually had a candle or something scented that would cover up most odors. (I did try to clean her box every week so that odor didn't become an issue.) But most people don't have that big of a bathroom. Or if they do have a master suite bathroom, they sure as hell don't want a litter box in the middle of their white and black harlequin marble floor.

My nephew used a spare half bath that was never occupied.
My sister used the laundry room for her cats.
I've seen litter boxes almost everywhere.
In a niche under the stairs.
In the basement.
In the garage.
Once, in a kitchen. (This made worse sense to me that the dining room.) I mean really, wouldn't that interfere with your cooking? "Dear? I think you might have a little too much ammonia in the pasta." (Though for a while I did keep a extra litter box in the kitchen for Krysla due to her issues with overnight visitors, but it was rarely used.)

I remember going thru the additives stage in the Seventies where it seemed like everyone was suggesting that you add *something* to the litter to help cover up the odor. There was baking soda. I thought snipping in grass clippings was more funny than practical (the idea was that the chlorophyll would help). Again, the easiest way to control the odor is to empty the box before stuff starts falling out of it. You don't want to wait until the handle on your plastic litter scoop snaps because the litter has formed one huge clump.

And this brings us back to why don't you just let Miss Prissy Paws go outside?

There are various reasons for not wanting your cat to go outside. You live downtown in a metropolitan city. Even if you live in some bedroom community thirty miles from heavy traffic, there are still the local idiots that won't slow down if your cat is crossing the street. (Or worse yet, they speed up.) It goes to forty below in the winter. There are coyotes outside that would love Miss Prissy Paws for dinner. The list is probably endless. So, whatever the reason, you have decided to have a litter box inside.

So deal with it. Empty the litter box every week (take out the trash? empty the litter box!). Then rinse the litter box out even if you use a liner. It takes fifteen seconds, so just do it.

For some reason, you chose to share your life with a cat and you have to deal with the consequences. Life stinks sometimes; litter boxes shouldn't.

The cat that played fetch.

Krysla was the cat who played fetch.

Which was surprising.

As I have said elsewhere in this book, Krysla wasn't a cat who liked to play games, or for that matter to play with cat toys. I think that may have come from the fact that, if she wasn't a feral kitty (I found her in a trash can), she had had a stunted upbringing. Not a lotta love in a house where someone puts the cat out with the garbage.

I had tried to interest her in cat toys, but nothing really caught her attention. The only "toy" she ever liked was the catnip filled mice, and those didn't last long. And besides, they were expensive. I was considering buying them in bulk.

One Sunday afternoon, I was sitting on the couch watching some TV. (Actually I had the TV on while I read the Sunday comics.) I was half asleep. It had been a rough week and though it was Sunday, I had gone in and worked that morning in the family business (sewing machines and vacuum cleaners; I caught up on the service work on Sunday). Krysla was asleep on the couch beside me. When I was cleaning up my late lunch, I crumpled up some aluminum foil, and shot it like a one inch basketball for the trash can beside the TV. I missed as usual. (I sucked at sports.)

There was a flash of fur and Krysla had the foil ball trapped on the floor between her two front paws. She hunkered over it. (*My precious.*)

And so the Great Foil Ball Fetch Games began.

Mostly on Sundays, when I was bored (really, really bored), I would wad up some foil and get Krysla to play fetch for a while. Well, at least *try* to get her to play fetch. I soon discovered, that even though I may have created the game (at least my half of it), it was Krysla who was the sole referee, umpire and line judge. She controlled the game better that Michael Jordan ever did.

We would start with short tosses, which she quickly got bored with going after. So, I got a little more imaginative and would bounce (by the way, foil does not bounce well) the ball off the wall and ricochet it in some unexpected direction. After a few times of doing this, Krysla would have it figured out and just wait for the ricochet, and *then* go after it. Each time she would bring the ball back to me clutched gently in her partially open mouth. It amazed me that she knew not to crush the ball. Maybe the foil just tasted bad.

But trying to bounce it took its toll on the aluminum ball. It flattened out on one side. Then it started to shrink as I had to squish it ever tighter to try to make it round again; until it finally became this slightly wet wad of compressed aluminum. By that time, I was ready to call it quits.

But not Krysla.

During the game, she would bring the ball back and drop it at my feet. When I had decided that the game was over, she would return the ball as usual and I would tell her, "No more. Game over. You win like always." She would stare at me, then at the ball. Sometimes she would even nudge the ball with her paw or nose. Then, if I hadn't picked the ball up in the time her little mind had allocated, she would pick the ball up in her teeth again. She would jump up on the sofa and proceed to walk slowly up to my chest. Once there, she would set the ball down again at her feet. If I still did not pick it up, she would grab it in her teeth again and step forward till the ball was right in front of my face. She would give me that look of, "You may have started this game, but I will tell you when it is over."

Just to get her off me without starting a hissy fit, I would take the ball again and throw it. Usually she would play the game a couple more rounds, but occasionally, she would walk over to the ball, sniff it, look back at me and without even returning the ball to me for the last time, she would casually walk away. Tail held high in an exclamation point.

I knew then that, "The game was over."

Your cat and the internet.

I have to say that I am not the biggest fan of putting cat pictures on the Internet.

That probably alienated a lot of people reading this simply because there are millions of kitty videos on a half dozen web sites plus god knows how many on Facebook pages; so obviously quite a few of you disagree with me.

When I managed a warehouse in Ohio, I can remember time being wasted with people watching and/or forwarding cat videos from this and that web page. Most of my employees knew I liked cats, and amazingly, some even forwarded videos to me. Kinda stupid, people. I'm the person that wrote the employee guidelines that say you aren't supposed to do that. Company computers are for company business. But that's sort of my point; those videos make people do stupid things. I mean, I even had employees of companies that we did business with sending me videos.

That was until those companies cracked down on non-business computer usage. They had to. Nationwide there were millions of man-hours being used to watch these things. And a lot of that time was on the company dime. Companies had to increase their computing capacities to handle non-business computer usage.

Now, I'm not saying that some of those videos weren't funny; some of them were hilarious because cats will do some weird things. (Even when they don't have stage mother owners trying to get them to do something cute so it can be posted online.) But there's a time and a place for everything.

Watching cat videos online is like eating potato chips; you really can't watch just one.

So, should you continue to keep posting stuff? Like I could stop you.

Since people have been trying to downsize families and are having less kids (I'm speaking in general terms, not specific families that you know), they are filling in for the non-existent kids with pets. So instead of Aunt Beatrice showing you pictures of all her nieces and nephews, she shows you pictures of Mr. Furry Britches and Princess Darling. And your sister absolutely must show you the video of her kid with her pets doing one thing or another that she took with her smart phone.

You can't avoid these things anymore.

It's just too easy to take pictures and videos. You have smart phones, and tablets and notebooks. There are digital cameras still floating around. You will see a digital video recorder every once in a while too. Soon, you will have some sort of digital phone on your wrist (in Texas you will have an option of putting them in a belt buckle).

As for your cat and YouTube; you shouldn't allow her to watch it. Cats have big enough egos anyway, why make them any bigger by giving them a new forum? Seeing themselves online will just make them more unbearable than usual.

What happens when you're not at home.

Have you given any thought to what happens when you're not at home? Ever wonder what that cute little furball does once the door closes behind you?

I think Krysla used to call her buddies over and have poker games. I would find poker chips under the sofa when I vacuumed. (of course, that might have been my roommate's). I would also find cheese puffs and occasionally a bra, which I am fairly certain, had nothing to do with Krysla. My one roommate did like to play strip poker.

When I would come home, she would always have that look on her face like she had gotten away with something. You know the look. Cats came up with the smug look. They asked God for it specifically when he was handing out attributes. They have that Mona Lisa smirk too; just a half smile to make you think. So, after I gave Krysla her scratching between the ears and fed her, I would just take a little walkabout in the house to see if she had left any evidence. I have to say she was good; I never found anything worth while.

I've mentioned elsewhere about leaving the TV on for your cat to watch. (I think it's stupid. You'll never fool her into thinking there's a human in the house. She can *smell* you know.) Then there is leaving cat toys out for her to play with while you're not there. Of course, if she won't play with them while you're home, what makes you think she'll do it when you're not there? Besides, how do you tell if she played with them? At least when Krysla got it on with her cat nip mouse, I knew about it because I would usually find the beheaded flannel corpse.

Of course, these days you can just set up a web cam, or five, and watch them on your computer at work. That should be easy enough to explain to your boss. You have time to watch the Kitty Surveillance Tapes (if it's not a category on YouTube already, then it will probably be an afternoon special on Fox TV) but you didn't finish the spreadsheet he needed by lunch. That should look good on your quarterly performance review. And if you do put up web cams, all you will probably see is a sleeping cat, or a cat eating a snack.

I think the easiest way to make sure that your cat is not hitting the Kitty Porn sites on your computer at home while you're away, is just get a second cat. They can wear each other out playing (or doing Zumba). Then they can socialize. (You know they *will* make lists of your short comings.) And now that I've made you slightly paranoid, you can check your credit card statements for any unusual purchases at the hardware store. They are sly little devils.

So, rather than drive yourself crazy, or come home to a crazy cat, get her a buddy to spend the day with while you're not there. If you don't want the second cat, then try to find a couple toys that will actually make her exercise a little. You know a springy toy you can mount in a rarely used doorway, or a ball in a ring she can bat around.

What do you mean there's someone else?

It's heartbreaking when you realize that your relationship with someone has changed, even if it's temporary.

She's not coming to meals on time.
You notice she is coming home from a different direction.
She just comes in, grabs a quick bite and then leaves.
She wants to stay out all night.
Then you catch them together.

Even though she's just a cat, it can still hurt.

Josey has a new buddy. (And yes, I probably need a real life.) It's odd, but I never realized that cats can have "friends."

I've mentioned there's a Tom that lives next door that looks enough like Josey he could be a litter mate. It's him. She's started hanging out with him. I have caught them sitting side by side having a quiet conversation a couple times now. It's so weird. I think of Josey as like any other cat, she's mostly solo. (Except when she's in heat, then she has an entourage that would put Tiger Woods to shame.) If we had another cat, she would probably be buddies with her/him. My friends used to have a dog too and Josey would sort of hang with him.

I know that cats socialize, but I've always thought that was only within a litter group, or some sort of family association. Not with a complete stranger. My friends in Ohio have always had a menagerie of cats, dogs, turtles and fish. I know other people that have equally diverse groups of pets. (My sister and nephew are one.) But again, that's what I consider a "family" group. You'll see dogs and cats nestled asleep together etc. but they have a common association of a group, and probably a scent thread that helps weave them together. That's expected.

What's different about Josey and Mr. Tom is that I don't know of any family connection. He's just the Tom next door. That's what makes it so unusual in my mind. I'm sure that whenever Josey would go into heat, Mr. Tom would be there knocking on the door and saying, "Hi. Maybe you've noticed me. I live just over there." He's probably the first in line. So how does a "friendship" develop between two neighboring cats that may have been hooking up occasionally?

We're dealing with cats, which probably put them at the human Neanderthal level; driven by instinct, but slightly civilized. So is it a case of "Ugh like Josey. Josey like Ugh?" or is it more complex than that?

What's even odder is why do I care?

Josey is just the cat that I share living space with most of the time. Yes, there is a basic emotional connection that humans have with dogs and cats (and maybe we want to include horses and dolphins in that). But that is the owner/pet relationship. I have seen way too many people say they "love" their pet and that the animal means everything to them. That in my mind is taking a feeling of fondness and moving it way too close to the edge of the abyss.

Okay, so I am fond of Josey. Am I jealous of the Tom next door suddenly having her attention instead of me? No. I am not jealous.

She's a *cat*!

I just found it odd that she was treating this non-familial cat like a friend. Maybe he *is* a long lost litter mate. At least she has someone to buddy with when I'm not around. She's a little more complex than I thought; closer to Cro-Magnon than Neanderthal.

.

To you my best feature is my armpit.

Josey loves my armpit.

Specifically, my left armpit (I don't know what's wrong with the right one, I got them as a matched set), and she can be pretty adamant about it. She will actually expend the energy to walk across me to get to the left one (and you know how cats are about using any energy that they don't absolutely have to use).

Krysla loved to be draped over my shoulders like a kitty shawl; back legs hanging down on one side of my neck, and head and front legs on the other side. She would have felt completely at home during more elegant times. Then, her other perch was sitting on just one shoulder. When she did that, I'd make a motion at her with one hand and say, "Kitty want a cracker?" (Cats really have mastered that look of total disdain, haven't they?)

I am not quite sure why Josey likes the armpit so much. Maybe because when she tucks herself in, lying on her side with her back paws and the left front paw in the armpit, she can drape the right front leg across the bend in my arm and lay her chin on my bicep. There, with her head just so, she can purr away, keeping me in sight. (In case I try any quick moves.)

Then there is the fact that my scent is probably well concentrated in my armpit due to sweat. (But that still doesn't explain why she prefers the left armpit.) Basically she just considers me one big meat pillow and will sit on me wherever she pleases. The armpit is obviously her comfort zone.

Krysla seemed to like lying between my legs when I was on my back for possibly the same reason. One girlfriend said it was a bit unnerving to be laying beside me and look down at my legs only to see a cat head rise from between my legs. (So many emasculating jokes come to mind that I will now ignore.) But since I can't sleep on my back, I would sometimes fall asleep that way, and then suddenly roll over on my side. Krysla would then be enveloped in a sheet and blanket burrito. She doesn't like Mexican and would let me know it. I would have to get everything rearranged while Krysla retreated to her backup position on her pillow.

As I said, Josey likes the armpit best, but she will move to sitting beside my head and rest her chin on my shoulder. (But then her whiskers tickle my face.)

Or she will sit on my chest when breakfast is late and she is trying to make a point. Or she will retreat to her blanket on the bottom corner of the bed if she is really pissed off. (Or it's just too hot lying right next to me.) And finally, if she has a real burr up her tail, she will get off the bed entirely and either goes under the dresser or downstairs on the sofa.

I've had another thought about her preference for my left armpit. Like most humans, my heart is on the left side of my chest. Maybe Josey can feel my heartbeat better on that side and it reminds her of being curled up next to her Mommy cat. Just a thought.

I like it best when she is curled up in my armpit. I hear her purring happily. I can look aside and see that cat smile on her face and know for a little while, all is good.

Got that lovin' feeling.

You'll know it when it happens.

It starts with that God-awful "mer-r-r-rowl-l-l-l" that crawls up and down your spine and lets every tomcat in the neighborhood know- kitty wants some lovin'!

I actually feel sorry for the female cats when they come into "season" or "heat". This is hormones on a rampage worse that any teenager ever has.

When Krysla and I shared a house that I was remodeling (or at least trying to fix up) and it had tons of windows. The house had a front porch that wrapped around my hexagonal bedroom over the front parlor. (Yes, houses actually had things called "front parlors".) The roof of the porch came up to within a foot of the bedroom windows.

Krysla would sit on the sill of the screened in window and just let loose like a Civil Air warning siren.
Day and night.
Night and day.

I remember coming home from work one day and the whole roof was literally (and I mean *literally*) covered in about thirty tomcats. Just waiting, grooming each other, with one eye always on the window. You could hear them murmuring dirty innuendos to each other about her.

"Yeah, Dude. She's gonna remember *me*. I'm gonna give it to her so bad."

"Bad is the operative word, I think."

"Well, Dude. She's gonna know when *I'm* done."

"They *always* know when we're done, Asshole."

And that is the sad part; the mating process is painful for the female because the male has a barb on his penis that lets her know he's done and is backing out. (Can't slip away like a coward like most males would do after a one night stand.) This also triggers the female cat to ovulate.

Krysla would slip out of the house somehow (she was one determined kitty), and lead a thundering herd of tomcats on a chase. Like the fox leading the hounds, she would drag their sorry asses all over the neighborhood before she gave up and let nature take its course. Over and over again, according to my irate neighbors.

"Your cat is at it *again!* She's practically servicing a half dozen toms at one time!"

"Would you *please* get your cat fixed?!"

"I had to explain to my daughter what the hell was going on."

"Really. Can't you do something about your cat? My cat isn't that way." (Your cat is one of the cats chasing my cat, Lady.)

As for the "walk of shame" when Krysla would arrive back the next morning (oh yeah, she would make a night of it most times), she would saunter up the street, tail held high. I would let her in, pet her, tell her she had been a very naughty kitty and then she would have a quick nosh and sleep the day away.

It wasn't that I didn't want to have her fixed. I just couldn't get her to the vet in time. She was actually getting pregnant before she had the first litter weaned. I finally took her in earlier than you are supposed to and explained to the vet. Her checked her and said he would do it.

So, no more air raid sirens, and no more kittens to find homes for. I was stuck with three cats for a while, but eventually I was down to just Krysla again.

Peace and quiet had descended on the kingdom.

I was happy. Krysla got fat.

I don't like your friends.

You ever get the feeling that your cat just flat out doesn't like your friends?

I mean, she doesn't dislike them so bad that she hisses immediately when one shows up, but instead she might give a little growl and doing that liquid fur thing cats can do, she flows silently away and disappears.

Various things can probably upset your cat.

One guy that I knew had dogs and Krysla would immediately take a dislike to him when he arrived. (Or maybe she just figured out he was an asshole before I did.) Any real strong scent, especially an acidic one like fertilizer, would send Krysla scurrying. Sometimes she would even give a sneeze before she took off and I figured that was just an allergic reaction to something on the visitor. (Or she could have been allergic to the person. How ironic; a cat allergic to human dander.) What a great excuse that could have been, "Oh, excuse me. You can't come in. My cat's allergic to you." But people in my hometown thought I was nuts already so I didn't want to push the issue too far.

A girl I knew (casual friend), swore her cat could judge the men that came to pick her up for a date. Could you imagine being that poor guy waiting at her door and not understanding why your date was looking at her cat while the cat was looking at you? Then finally being told, "Nope. Sorry. This isn't going to work. Miss Furball says so." Man, if that didn't deflate your ego nothing would. How would you tell your friends that you never got past her front door because you didn't pass her cat's criteria? (You wouldn't. You'd be a man about it and lie and make like you dumped her.)

Is it really that important that your friends get along with your cat?

Do you really have a death wish?

Or at the least, do you want a shoe full of cat piss? Well, maybe not *your* shoe. I have heard of an episode where people were at a girl's house for a party and saw the owner's cat walk up and take a pee on a guy. That just could not go over well. I mean a cat just strolling thru the crowd and picking this one guy out to urinate on. Yes, I'm sure it was funny as hell to everyone but the guy. I have to wonder if the cat's owner and the guy had some previous history. I find cats to be selective in their vengeance.

Basically it boils down to this; if your cat doesn't like your friends, you either have to find a way to bridge that gap, or change the cat's mind. (Though it might be easier to just find new friends.)

So, if you are the recipient of a cat's dislike and it looks like it will be worth the effort (the girl is smart, and cool and really hot) of getting on the cat's good side to make a relationship with the owner possible; then make the effort. I suggest finding out what the cat's favorite crunchies are and have some in your pocket. Offer them to the cat as soon as it arrives to check you out. You might want to bring the girl something too.

(Not crunchies.)

Thank you for the warm spot.

It's a cool, almost a cold day. You've been in bed reading with your cat sleeping beside you. The cat doesn't even open an eye partway when you get up to empty your bladder. But when you come back, she has miraculously levitated herself over into the warm spot you had made and is sound asleep again.

You *really* weren't gone that long. How the hell did a sleepy cat move that fast?

Cats must have heat sensors like pit vipers because they can always find the warmest spot on a cold day, and conversely they can find the coolest place out of the blazing sun. (Except for sunbeams; sunbeams are a special case.)

I think part of this is determined by the "lazy" gene that all cats have. (This is an animal that normally sleeps 15 hours a day; of course it has a "lazy" gene.) Cats can be very energetic. If you have ever watched a cat tearing up the grass hunting down the wild and ferocious Common Gray Squirrel in your backyard, you know what I mean. But besides the occasional backyard safari by your domestic cat, they eat and they sleep.

The "lazy" gene, as I call it, is a gene that evolution has given the cat to maximize its sleeping time.

This special adaptation by domestic cats allows them to make the best use of any down time in their day. Why do you think a "cat nap" by humans is about fifteen to thirty minutes long? That is the optimum time a cat needs for the minimum recharge of its batteries. That cat nap enables the cat to get from its napping spot, to its food bowl to check for any crunchies it might have missed at mealtime, and then get back to its napping spot. At that point, the lazy gene kicks in and Miss Kitty is down for the count; KO'd by its biology.

This is why the warm spot is so important.

Without its human companion pre-warming a spot for its nap, a cat (even with a highly developed lazy gene) cannot maximize the sleep potential it has on any given day. Now, it is my belief that thru the constant contact of human and cat over the centuries, the "lazy" gene has been partially absorbed by humans (especially human males) and comes out in the previously mentioned "cat nap".

This is a symbiotic relationship from which the cat seems to benefit the most. And cats being the smart animals they are, and if they could speak, they would thank you for the warm spot.

Now I need a cat nap after writing this.

Hairball!

There is nothing like stepping on a wet hairball in your bare feet. Nothing.

You heard the horrendous hacking and vomiting sound mixed with the coughs that you have come to know as - *hairball*!
You get out of bed, walking around looking for the cat.
You've been turning on lights but you're half asleep.
You don't see it in time and suddenly it's underfoot.

If you took a piece of liver and wrapped it in wet fur, you might come close to the feeling under foot. It's wet and squishy; especially if it's on the tile. It gets a little lost in carpet.

Why, you say, don't I wait till morning? Have some coffee, a toasted bagel with a smear, and *then* look for the hairball? Because mornings are usually a panic with my friends; one coming home from work, the other leaving. And the cat is basically my responsibility now.

Plus, I just worry that it might be something else other than a hairball. Ok, that sounds a little pathetic, but I don't have a lot going on in my life right now and the cat brings me a little happiness. So I worry about things like hairballs.

They actually aren't that big of deal. I give Josey a hairball food mixture (most companies make one) and make sure she has fresh water in her bowl all the time. Josey is a short hair tabby, so her hairballs aren't that frequent. Long hair cats (like Bubba Kitty) are more prone to them, so you should groom long haired cats to help deal with them.

However, this is not a cat maintenance manual; it's a cat/human relationship book filled with my opinions and observations.

So let's get back to just how disgusting a hairball feels under the arch of your bare foot.

I think it's the contrast between dry foot and wet hairball that really sets it off. It's the maximum "Ew-w-w" factor. And the wetness is from her saliva and mucus and has the stickiness that no one but a horror film director would like. Remember the stuff dripping from the jaws of the creatures in "*Alien*"? Yeah, that stuff.

Whatever.

If you have a cat in your life, get used to hairballs, because like runny noses on kids, they are part of your life now.

Two cats or one? (But never a dozen.)

I am not sure of the character's real name, but on *The Simpsons* there is a crazed older woman that is always surrounded by, and throwing, cats. I think they call her the *Crazy Cat Lady*. On another show, there is the neighbor lady who has what she affectionately calls her "brood" of probably a dozen cats.

Why are crazy people on TV and in movies always shown to have dozens of cats? Is the having a large number of cats a symptom of some weird disease? *Multicatsihaveia*? Will at some point *all* cat owners be struck down by this horrible disease? I guess it's just trying to show that it's odd having a lot of one thing. (Cats, kids, wives – it's the basis of a lot of reality shows.) Like the person is hoarding cats.

Now I've known several people that have had multiple cats. *I* had multiple cats at one point. *My sister* had multiple kitties. *My best friend* had multiple felines. *Several ex-girlfriends* had multiple cats. *Most farms* that have cats probably have multiple cats. So the case for insanity based on having more than one cat is pretty thin. Maybe you have to have at least a dozen cats for it to be a part of the description of nuts. Let's go with that, if you have a dozen cats or more (and don't live on a farm), then you might need to talk to a doctor about it. Love of any animal or thing can only go so far, and then it has to be considered a little extreme.

So what are the good reasons for having multiple cats in your house?

I have always felt that if you or you and your spouse and/or family are gone all day, then that is a good reason to have two cats. The little beasties keep each other company, give themselves someone to play with, someone to socialize with while you are gone. That's a good thing. That way when you come home, you aren't greeted by a solitary cat that has a lot of anxiety built up. You want to come home and be met by a happy cat that will greet you with purring and leg rubs, not a cat that has spent the day peeing in every one of your shoes.

So is there any good reason for having more than two cats? What if you have three kids? If you only had one cat, you could use the "We have one pet that we all share" routine. But if you have two cats, why can't you have three? (This is the slippery slope.) You could give in, but you have set the precedent that the kids don't have to share. Plus two cats might share one litter box, but my personal experience is that getting three cats to share is doubtful. (You are also cleaning the litter box every three days.) And good luck with getting the kids to empty the litter box. ("What? I took out the clumps that my cat did. The other stuff is from Billie and Emma's cats.") You are in deep doo-doo when crap gets personalized.

To simplify it all, my personal feeling is that two cats per household are enough.

If you want a dozen of something, buy donuts.

When your cat is an addict.

When I lived with Krysla back in the Seventies, I would occasionally give her a catnip filled fabric toy. It was usually in the shape of a mouse.

Within hours, I would find the decapitated head of the toy.

After a careful search, I would find Krysla with the body of the toy clenched between her two front paws with her nose buried in the neck of the carcass happily snorting on the contents. We are talking Tony Montana from the end of "*Scarface*" level of snorting. However, the paranoid look on Tony's face was replaced with the complacent mellowness of Bill Murray as the assistant groundskeeper in "*Caddy Shack*". Krysla was so-o-o content that nothing could harsh her mellow. She would be useless for several hours. (My roommate had a similar condition during the Sixties and Seventies.)

If however, you tried to remove the toy from her paws- bad idea. One bleary eye would open slightly and from the depths of hell (Or her throat.) a low growl like you had never heard and would never want to hear again, would be emitted. After that, I would usually just leave her to it until she would stagger out to the kitchen for a long drink from her bowl. Then I would grab the saliva soaked toy, put it in a plastic bag and stuff it down in the garbage. By this time she was distracted looking for some crunchies to calm her voracious appetite. (Again, not unlike my roommate.)

The toys were expensive unless I bought them in bulk. Then I remembered that my mom had a catnip plant in her garden. So I went up and took a large plug of the plant and transplanted it in a cool spot along my front porch among the azaleas.

It was a mistake planting it along the porch which was only a couple feet from the sidewalk.

Krysla quickly discovered the plant. At first, she would just lie down beside the plant and occasionally take a sniff; much like a gentleman sniffing his brandy before taking a sip.

As the plant grew, she would rub her whole head against it. And if any of the neighbor cats would be sniffing around, she would growl and hiss and quickly send them on their way. (*My precious.*)

Later, when the plant was larger still, I would see her leave the plant with a sprig of it dangling from her mouth. (Maybe it had gone out and she was looking for a light.)

And finally, like a reveler in a Roman orgy, I would find her rolling her whole body in the plant. Then she would sprawl on her back, spread eagled with her centerline showing to the whole world. (Man, I never realized how much she was like my old roommate until now.)

As the summer passed, I would be sitting on my porch working on one of my motorcycles. A little girl that lived in the neighborhood would be walking past and stop, looking at Krysla. Then the kid would look at me and ask, "Is your kitty sick, Mister?" And I would shake my head and tell her that the kitty was just really tired. (Just like her dad was after watching Sunday football.)

Then on another Sunday another kid would pass, look at the cat and say, "Hey Buddy. I think your cat's dead." I would look over the side of the porch, wiping my greasy hands on a rag and declare. "Nope. See. She's breathing." The kid would leave and I would get back to the bike.

Finally, towards the end of summer I would get the occasional call from some neighbor down the street complaining that I had a dead cat laying in my yard and would I dispose of it. I would try to explain that said cat was just stupefied, not dead. At which point I would usually hear a religious reference of some sort and then the dial tone.

But when I came home and Animal Control was parked in my driveway and the officer was poking Krysla with a stick, I decided the plant finally had to go. So I dug it up and threw it away.

Krysla actually mourned the loss. She would sit by where the plant had been and sniff, hoping that there was still one last sprig in the ground. I swear if she could have, she would have left a wreath of flowers there.

Watch out down below! (Cats in high places.)

Cats like to be in high places.

We've all seen the cat stuck in the tree. Sometimes this draws ridiculous attention. The local TV crew and the fire department get there "To rescue the kitty", and just before she is "rescued" she runs down the trunk of the tree like the Roadrunner in a cartoon and leaves everyone looking like idiots.

People, believe me, that cat is gonna come down when she is hungry enough. Unless her life is in danger for some reason (Power lines etc.), just let nature take its course.

But what about in your home?

Cats actually need high places to feel comfortable and safe. A cat "tree" is a good idea if you have the room for one. You've seen them in a friend's house or a pet store. They're usually made of wood and have different carpeted levels that a cat can step or jump to as it maneuvers around on it. They don't have to be fancy, just sturdy. And most of the time, a scratching post covered in rope has been made out of the center pole. This lets kitty clean her claws and mark the cat tree as her territory. (Actually, your whole house is her territory. You just don't know it, but she does.)

How many times have you had to tell your cat to "get down" from a fireplace mantle or on top of a piece of furniture? Then there is the whole process of "cat proofing" your house. I have lost too many glass vases, knick knacks etc from when a cat gets its head easily past an item on a shelf, but forgets about the doublewide trailer they're pulling behind. Then you run in from the other room looking to see what happened (like you didn't know) and there's kitty just looking at the mess on the floor with a "how on earth did that happen?" look on its face. (However, I have gotten rid of a couple atrocious gifts that I blamed on the cat knocking off the shelf. Not proud about this, but God they were ugly.)

Cats need a path above floor level to be able to move around a room without touching the floor. Give them a way to move from the floor to the sofa, from the sofa back to the cabinet, from the cabinet to a bookcase, from the bookcase to a table and back down to the floor. This makes them feel safe. This way they can get away from any floor bound danger. (*Dog, Will Robinson. Dog.*) A friend's cat loved to work its way up into a book case where it would sit/lie in a gap between the books on a shelf like a bookend. It was tucked in and could survey its kingdom. (*It's all mine. I just allow you to live here.*)

But you need to watch where you place certain items. One friend had a bookcase near his front door and it seemed like every time I came in, that damn cat would be there and take a swipe at me. Luckily he was declawed so I got a soft slap instead of a set of razor sharp claws across the face.

Having a room organized for a cat to do a walk-about is good, but I've seen it done to extremes. I remember seeing a couple on TV that had made walkways around the ceilings of all the rooms in their house, with holes cut in the walls so their cats could pass from one room to the next. They even had a set of steps going from behind a sofa up the wall to a walkway. It looked sorta cool but also sorta borderline crazy.

When my nephew lived in the log cabin, his cat Tigger was in heaven with all the cross beams of logs and natural ledges the logs made. These provided perfect walkways and hidey holes for him.

The other thing cats like to do is look outdoors. They can see nature in action, but they don't have to dirty their paws in it. Putting a hummingbird feeder outside the window will really get your cat's attention. One person in a TV show had a cat door in an unused basement stairs door that led to a wired in enclosure with walkways and even a little water feature with a bubbler pump and goldfish to entertain his cat (and yes, the fish kept disappearing). He even had a mini tree house for his cat so she could get out of the sun.

Krysla loved the bay windows and wide window sills in the painted lady. If you have wide sills on a window, make it cat available so your kitty can sit and watch the birds and squirrels outside. If you do these things ahead of time, you'll save yourself a lot of grief later when your cat makes his own way to the windows. Cats can be like furry mini bulldozers when they set their minds to it.

Your cat needs to feel safe in your house as much as you do. Whether you realize it or not, you share your home with an intelligent resourceful animal (and yes, I'm not talking about your spouse).

Yes, you are a little pill. (My cat the drug pusher.)

A little pill. It's what my grandmother used to call me when I was being a pest. When I asked what did that meant, she said I was little and a pain in the neck. I probably was.

Josey is also a "pill" and she has found an interesting way to show it.

It started several months ago. Josey came into my room first thing in the morning. As usual, she wanted her breakfast. I looked at the clock on the nightstand and it was probably 4 or 5am. I was not ready to get up yet, so I just rolled over on my side and pulled the pillow close so I could go back to sleep. Josey sat there for a little while just watching me try to fall asleep. Eventually, she walked over me and jumped up on the desk beside my bed.

My desk is a mess. There are prescription receipts that I haven't filed yet, miscellaneous bills that need paid or have been paid and need filed, a clock radio and an old CD boom box, a table lamp and bottles of pills. Lots of bottles of pills: about a dozen meds that keep me chugging along. I have them neatly in line and separated between morning and evening. They are about a foot from the edge of the desk.

On the desk, Josey sits on her haunches and continues to look at me. But one morning, she did something different. I have a small travel pill box that contains my early morning pills. It's plastic and when there are pills in it, it will rattle when you shake it. Of course, Josey can't pick it up and shake it, but she can swat it like she does her toy rattle balls and it makes a very similar noise.

So, that morning I'm laying there trying to fall back asleep and Josey is sitting there with her stomach grumbling. In frustration, boredom or for some other reason, Josey decided to swat my early morning pill box. It slid and dropped over the edge of the desk and onto the floor. I watched as she walked over to the edge and looked down. Then she went back and started to push another pill bottle around. I thought enough is enough and told her "no". That stopped her for a moment, and then she started up again. I got up and pushed her off the desk as I told her "no" once again.

There wasn't a repeat of this behavior for a while, then one morning I didn't get up fast enough to suit her and she started again. I would say "no" and she would stop. Soon she was just ignoring me and I would get up as soon as the first bottle went over the edge.

I guess I had become Josey's Pavlovian dog, reacting just the way she wanted me to.

Finally it came to a standoff one morning. She had pushed the first bottle of pills off the desk and I just lay back in bed. (I was having a bad morning with a lot of pain.) Then she pushed another bottle over the edge and I said "no". She waited a moment to see if I got up and I didn't, so she pushed another bottle off. I stayed put. So another bottle met its doom. Then another. Then another. I refused to budge and just said "no" between each bottle.

That morning, Josey worked her way through my complete collection of medications. Maybe twelve bottles were forced to jump by this feline pill killer, each with a small pause in between. Instead of getting Josey to bend to my will, I had created a serial pill bottle pusher. When she was out of pills, she looked around and then headed for my cell phone and that was when I reached out and grabbed my phone. I stayed in bed for a while and Josey finally got off the desk and went to her towel on the corner of the bed. She sat there with her front paws tucked under her breast and glared at me.

The lesson here is that it is very hard to get a cat to do what you want. They work on a very simple structure of cause and reaction. By jumping up when this first started and then immediately feeding her, I made a mistake. I set up a cause / reaction situation that was exactly what *she* wanted and *not* what I wanted.

I no longer get up right away and Josey has stopped (for the time being at least) in pushing the pill bottles to their doom.

Wait a minute. I just heard a pill bottle hit the floor.

Crap! *She's ba-a-a-ack.*

Cats in business suits. (Do bookstores attract cats?)

Really; do bookstores attract cats, or is it just coincidence?

I have to say that in almost (if not all) the small bookstores I've been in, they have had a least one "store cat." I mean, I think its cool that they do. I will walk into my local place and there's this big furball, (never little small framed cats; it's always big bruisers), lying sprawled on the check out counter, or in amongst the stacks of new releases (under the elevated section in the middle so the cat can reach a paw out for you just as you reach for a book).

In my case, I will usually just reach over absentmindedly and give him a scratch behind an ear and walk on. Other people will come in and make a meal of it.
Talking to the cat.
Petting the cat.
Asking how it feels.

Even asking what it thinks of *this* book as they hold some new tome in front of the cat's face. (Thankfully, most times the cat will give a disgusted look of "Are you kidding me?" at this maneuver and close his eyes as if to shut out the stupidity.)

Or if the cat isn't in sight, they will ask if "He's not in today?" like the cat has set hours and clocks in and out with the other employees. (He don't need no stinking time card.)

It's a *cat*, people, not the accountant.

I can understand the fact that a lot of bookstores owners are cat people. Book readers tend to be introverts and so do cat owners. Interestingly, I can't remember seeing a dog in a bookstore. I'm sure there are some; I've just never seen one. Perhaps they need too much attention whereas a cat can entertain itself. (That's usually by watching the antics of the customers.) But a cat in a bookstore just fits in. It's like a hot mug of cocoa in front of a fireplace on a winter's eve. Its just part of the cozy scene: a Norman Rockwell moment. Something you would have seen on the cover of *Life* magazine.

Normally the cat is just a quiet presence, a part of the background. I think the cat being there helps with the store's *vibe*. It makes the store feel more like you're at a friend's house checking out what new book he got instead of being in a business. It's a good marketing idea. If a person feels de-stressed they will spend more time in the store and that means a better chance of a sale.

The best use of this would be a store that had a permanent display of cat related books on a table and in the elevated center section was a small blanket (And a throne would be nice.), where the store cat would hold audience if he was so disposed.

And it's probably good for the cat. Cats are social animals and though they would probably prefer the company of their own species, the company of humans will do in their place.

Barn cats. Farm cats.

At the other end of the spectrum from cats in business suits are the barn cats or generally all farm cats.

Farm cats are working cats for the most part.

I dated a girl in junior high and her family had a farm. She always showed goats and horses at the county fair (she was a 4H girl), so I had expected to see those, but they also had some dairy cows and a couple bulls. The real business of their farm was raising grain for feed. You know; corn, wheat, oats, soy beans, that kind of stuff. When I visited her at her place one Saturday, I noticed several cats wandering around. I made the mistake of saying something about her "Having a lot of pet cats." She laughed. "Those aren't pets. Though I think the white one is pretty. Those are what Dad calls the tiny livestock." "The useless livestock is more like it," her brother chimed in as he walked past. "You're the useless one here, "She hollered back at him.

Thus began my education about farm cats. (I was desperate to find something to talk to her about. I knew squat about farm animals, but I knew some things about cats.) As we went around the farm, she was doing her regular chores and I was "helping" her with them. (It probably made the chores twice as long to do with my help.) She explained that the cats almost never went in the house. Her mom gave in once when the momma cat was pregnant in the middle of winter and let her have the kittens inside. But then the momma cat moved all the kittens back to the barn and none of them survived the winter. I asked if she buried the kittens. "Nope. Something probably ate them. They just disappeared one by one as the winter went on."

Such was the life of a barn cat. The momma cat just kept getting pregnant and having kittens. Some of them survived and some didn't. They didn't feed the cats; they ate mice and voles and whatever they could catch. Eventually the momma cat would die and maybe one of her kittens would take over. Some times the farms would have too many cats (all the cats would breed with each other regardless of who was related to whom) and then there would be a harsh winter and nature would correct for the over-population. When the snow melted you would find the remains of the cats that didn't make it.

My dad's business had a booth at several county fairs every summer and fall, so I ran into 4H kids a lot. I heard various stories about farm cats. Some were like the first girl's farm; the cats survived on what they caught. They weren't pets at all.

They were barn cats. Other kids (mainly girls; you think I would talk to the guys about cats?) might have one cat that lived in the house and that was a pet. But then they would have barn cats too, and the farm cats were on their own. Only a couple girls actually just had a pet cat. There were no cats around on their farms.

I came to realize that the kids that had farm cats were usually the farms that had cattle, horses, sheep and goats. The farms that didn't have barn cats raised pigs or chickens. The cattle and horse farms had a lot of grain that mice liked, so the cats were beneficial to the farm in keeping the rodent population down. The pig and chicken farmers had feed that was less appealing to the mice, so cats weren't really needed. Those farms usually had several dogs instead.

Cats came over on the ships from Europe. I wouldn't be surprised if there had been cats on the Mayflower. Domestic cats weren't native to the New World so they had to have come with the settlers. They undoubtedly came for the same reasons; to control rodent populations. Most ships had cats for that reason.

Cats and farms have been interconnected since the time of the Pharaohs, when cats were first domesticated, and for the same reason. Rats and mice ate the grains that farmers harvested for themselves. Cats ate the rats and mice. (Hopefully *before* they got to the grain bins.) It's a relationship that has benefited everyone in its circle.

Now, I'm sure that there are many more cats that are pets in homes than there are working cats on farms. But let's not forget that cats helped Mankind civilize the whole world. So, pet your kitty and say thank you and she'll look up at you and reply, "It's about damn time."

Girls that dress up as cats on Halloween (And the guys that want them to dress up as cats).

Okay the women reading this are already rolling their eyes, and any guys that might be reading this are starting to wet their lips in anticipation. Both of you; get over it!

Every Halloween you will find at least one girl dressed as a cat. Guaranteed.

It starts out with just the cat ears and maybe drawn on whiskers. On a Tween this is "cute". Then as the girl gets older, the costumes get bolder. The teenager with the cat ears, whiskers, a tail and a leopard print leotard starts getting as slutty as possible (and she's joined by her friends dressed as slutty nurses, slutty cops, slutty just about everything). Then later it becomes the soccer mom trying to prove that she still has it and she's wearing the full cat outfit with black leggings and long black gloves ending in clawed cat paws. Finally, we get to the MILF dressed in a leopard print coat (or the real thing) and she has nothing to prove. You can even extend it to the *Playmates* that get a cat costume painted on their naked bodies at a *Playboy Mansion* party.

One of the most popular Broadway play ever? *Cats!*

And what did the caveman want to see his mate dressed up in? *Sabertooth!*

When I was a teenager and out dating, I loved the moment when I realized my date didn't have just plain old white briefs on, but leopard printed bikini panties. And when a girl had that first chance to break away from plain white, or plain pink, and jumping past the printed little flowers, she would choose the spotted bikini panties. I asked a girl once what the fascination with cats, and especially with leopard prints, was. She said her mom would be watching TV and some Hollywood star would be wearing a leopard skin coat. Her dad would mention how good the star looked. The girl said it was obvious that her parents thought the star looked sexy; they just would never come out and say it. (At least, not in front of their daughter.) It was as if the desire to be dressed as a cat was passed down thru the generations.

I think that people think cats are sexy because of how they move.

Cats shoulders are not fixed in place like ours, they move independently. First the right one up, then the left one up. That is what makes cats look so slinky and I think guys transfer that motion to the way girls walk; first the right hip up slightly, then the left one up. What gives a cat the slink to its walk, gives a girl the sexy to her walk.

Whatever, I'm sixty and I honestly can't remember a time when there wasn't a girl dressed up as a cat at Halloween.

And God bless their little hearts for doing it.

Location. Location. Location.

Cat's have special spots for everything.

There's one place they can catch the best sunbeam.
There's another that's nice and cool on a hot summer day.
There's another where they feel extra safe and can watch the neighbor's dog.
Then they know when he's taken inside and can safely go outside for their own little stroll about the catdom.
There's a spot to keep an eye on the squirrel that will one day find its way to the ala carte menu.
There's the spot under the pines for the outdoor latrine on nice days and the spot under the camellias for shelter on not so nice days.
There's the spot on the cool pavement under the car on hot days.

And then there are the very special spots; it's nap time and where oh where should I go?

These spots form a round robin at the very core of a cat's daily routine. The nap is second only to food (female cat) or sex (male cat).

There are the obvious spots.
My favorite chair that's been empty all day, but now it's right before my favorite show on TV.
On top of the girlfriend's favorite afghan when she's not feeling well.
Under any of the dining room chairs as we're setting the table for dinner.
In my girlfriend's underwear drawer.
On top of the top loading DVR on movie night.
On my girlfriend's pillow.
On top of the book my girlfriend has been trying to find all day so she could finish the last chapter before book club that night.
On top of your car keys as you're rushing around in the morning.
On top of your phone. (This is easy to solve. Leave your phone on vibrate and call it to find it. Just wait for the loud "Meow!")

Other than my girlfriend's pillow ("Why doesn't she ever use *your* pillow? Huh? It's always *mine*."), there are other special places in the bedroom. Josey is particularly fond of the bedroom for naps.

There is on Josey's towel (which is her blankey and god forbid you ever use it for anything else) on the bottom corner of the bed. Again, has to be on the girlfriend's side of the bed. She's shorter than me, so there's more room for it.

I had a waterbed when Krysla was around. She preferred the spare pillow first, but if deposed from that throne, she used to use the space in the middle top of the bookcase headboard. She would sprawl there with one paw dangling over the edge like a fisherman on a pier trying fruitlessly to catch something. She also liked that spot when I was lucky enough to be having sex in the waterbed. I'd make sure she wasn't there when things started heating up, but damned if she wasn't always there for the finish; which tended to freak the women out. (I hear from friends that have dogs that dogs like to watch too.)

There's the spot under the dresser for when Josey is mad at me. She will crawl under there and make sure her back is to me to show her disdain.

Now when she's really feeling insecure (and maybe a little paranoid), she somehow squeezes her way back behind some cartons of papers and books near the computer. I only know she's back there because if I come close, she hisses. Couldn't figure out how she knew it was me until I was down on all fours looking for something on the floor. Then I just happened to be able to see two green eyes looking at me from between two boxes. Sneaky, paranoid kitty.

And if her tail is twitching, I just leave her to nap wherever she has decided to sleep. If you look real close, her eyes are open just a hair. But it's enough for her to get your range for a good swipe if you come closer.

You may *have* to let sleeping dogs lie, but I leave napping cats to their kitty dreams by choice.

I choose not to be scratched, kicked and hissed at.

Oh, yeah. Right there. That's the spot.

Cats definitely react differently to where you rub them and how hard. (Not unlike an ex-girlfriend who I always seemed to rub the wrong way. Hence the "ex" part.)

Most people will pat a cat on the head when they first meet the animal. This is usually a sign that that person is not a cat owner or even, horrors of horrors, not a pet person at all. You pet dogs; you stroke a cat. Or you can scratch one in the sense of a "You're sitting in the easy chair and you just casually without thinking scratch your stomach because it feels good." sort of scratch; not like "You have eczema and want to rip your skin off. " type of scratch.

There is one difference I want to explain; "scratching" is done with your nails, while "rubbing" is done with your finger tips. There is a big difference between them to a cat. "Stroking" can be done with just your fingers or your whole hand. These are my definitions not some pet owners manual definition.

When I first meet a cat, I stretch out my hand and let the animal sniff and/or even lick my fingers. Because my hands touch me generally everywhere, they pick up scent signals that the cat interprets and attaches to my image.

But cats have particular spots they like to have scratched, stroked and generally rubbed. And they have spots you do NOT want to do any of those things to. Get out the bandages if you do.

Krysla loved the under the chin scratch and the behind the left ear rub. Those were her favorites. If she was really feeling love for you, she would lie on her back showing her centerline (this is "I give up; you win." in cat speak) and let you rub her tummy. But it had to be a special occasion (your birthday or on Christmas, or on Hanukah for Deb) and don't rub too long because you can wear out your welcome here real quick. Actually, a cat can decide in a split second that you have been attached to one spot too long. She will either shift you to another spot by moving her body so you now have access to that spot, or decide "Obviously you don't know what you're doing and for where you are touching me, I want a professional masseuse." and get up and leave. Cats are the masters at the huffy walkaway. (That's why, from the back, their tails look like an exclamation mark, or an uplifted finger.)

Now you need to know that cats have scent glands in their cheeks and under their chin. These glands give off pheromones that help Miss Kitty mark her territory, or in this instance, mark you as part of her territory. So when you rub your cat under the chin or on her cheeks, you transfer her scent to you. This is a *good* thing.

She also can leave her scent by urinating. This would be a *bad* thing.

When you rubbed Smoker under the chin, he would get a case of the "cat giggles" and fall over backwards. This was Smoker's response to almost any stimuli. He was my George Carlin. My Cheech. But I loved him anyway. And it wasn't his fault.

Bubba Kitty was an attention slut when I was around. He would roll on his back and show his centerline to anyone. He was "easy." But Bubba Kitty and I had a special relationship, and Bubba Kitty had his special spots too. Like all cats, once he got to know you, he loved being scratched under the chin. The behind the ear rubs were also good for him. For me, he just loved me to stroke him on the top of his head, from the bridge of his nose back thru his ears to the nape of his neck. He had a skin condition and the top of his head seemed to be the one place that wasn't affected.

Then there's Josey. Josey is very temperamental about her affections. She was a feral kitty and has that standoffish aloofness that all undomesticated animals have. Now this is how she reacts to me. I'm sure as with all cats, she reacts to different humans in her life in different ways. We humans do the same thing; we have friends, relatives and people we can't stand to even be with in the same room. It's human nature. It's also cat nature.

Now, this is how she reacts to me. Josey loves the "under the chin" and its close cousin, the "rub my cheeks" rubbing. She gets that closed eyes blissed look on her face when I do it correctly, and the eyes open a slit when I haven't quite hit the right spot yet. (Guys you've seen this same reaction in your girlfriend under certain conditions. Just transfer that knowledge.) She reacts the same way to the "nose rub". Starting just where her nose meets her fur and rubbing back between her eyes then her ears. She'll arch her neck to keep me rubbing the right place.

That's when you know, "Oh yeah. Right there. *That's* the spot."

Cats in retirement.

You see them more and more in retirement and nursing homes; cats in repose, helping themselves to the good life in retirement.

These are what I call attention sluts. They don't care who gives them a pat, or a scratch under their chin. It's just, come on baby, give it to me. But they are doing something important; they are helping others.

There was a nursing home attached to the apartment complex where I lived for twenty years. I would have to go over there for one reason or another (Something would need fixed in my apartment.), and I noticed the cats in residence. There were a couple big (Overweight.) kitties walking around like they owned the place. They seemed to have access to all the common areas. One tabby would wander by, weaving in and out around the chairs and couches where the residents sat. You would see an elderly resident (I used to call them "Lollies" for "Little Old Lady".) gently reach down and pet the cat as it passed. Another time you would see one jump up on the couch and meow at a Lollie and she would talk right back to the cat. Then the cat would jump down and resume its patrol among the army of legs at its disposal.

I thought it was interesting that the nursing home would have posters up that would tell the residents about dogs being brought in for them to pet, etc., but the cats lived in. The dogs visited; the cats were residents. I never saw a Lollie mistreat a cat. No yelling about "Get that damn thing away from me." They just accepted the felines as part of the household.

My mother ended up in a different nursing home in her last three years. Mom had Alzheimer's (which I wouldn't wish on my worst enemy) and when I went to visit, I noticed they had cats. Hilariously, they also had this huge bird cage full of parakeets and other colorful small birds that the Alzheimer patients seemed to enjoy. (I know my Mom did.) I remember one day coming in to see Mom and I found her sitting on a bench opposite the bird cage. There was a big cat (again overweight; I guess the residents would slip treats to the kitties), sitting beside Mom on the bench. Mom was telling the cat which bird was which and having a good old conversation with the cat. When I got to them, the cat gave me a reproachful look like I wasn't coming around enough (and I wasn't) and then the cat slid off the bench to continue its rounds while I chatted with my Mom.

One visit, my mom looked troubled. When I asked if something was wrong, I expected a reply concerning the food or one of the other residents or something like that. Nope. Mom was worried because she went to empty the litter box for the cat and she couldn't find the box anywhere. I explained that they were the nursing home cats and she didn't have to worry about their litter box. She was relieved. Then she leaned close and said, "That's good, because I don't think I've been remembering to feed them either."

I think the cats, in their own special way, made Mom's last years a little more pleasurable, and most certainly less lonely. It's good to know that some cats have their own special purpose in life.

I remember reading an article about a cat at a nursing home that would go in and sleep on a resident's bed instead of its normal sleeping spot. During the night that the cat was present, the resident would pass on and head towards the light at the end of their tunnel of life. During the Middle Ages, that would have gotten that cat burned alive for witchcraft. Today, it's just a small item used as news filler.

Cats are special. Don't ever forget that. They have become woven into humankind's tapestry of events, into our very psyche. It will be a sad day indeed if that thread ever becomes unwoven with us.

Walking cats on a leash.

I've actually seen this happen in someplace other that a circus or a late night TV show: a cat on a leash. I can hear the cats watching this event thinking, "What the hell are you doing Buddy? We don't do leashes."

Why would someone want to walk a cat on a leash?

Really, just think about it. Cats are the free spirits of the domestic animal kingdom. We all like to watch them run and jump, and play with stuff, so why on earth would we want to tie them down with a leash? You put animals on a leash when you want to control them. Dogs seem to actually like being on a leash (choker chains excluded) and will trot along beside you when you walk. I personally think that cats are just too damn inquisitive to be contained. Cats want to stop and smell stuff, and explore as they go along. Dogs, for the most part, just don't seem to have that same level of curiosity. You will never hear someone say that curiosity killed the dog. (Flatulence maybe, but not curiosity.)

I can understand trying to have a cat on a leash if you live in an apartment complex or a condo where the rules say that all pets that are outside must be on a leash. (There are a lot of control freaks that write just such rules.) You want your cat to be able to go outside, so you try a leash. Unless you started that cat on a leash when it was a small kitten, I don't see you having much success with that. Instead, you will probably end up with a small tornado of pissed off energy on the end of that leather strap. And if you used one of those leashes that are on a reel, you would end up looking like you were trying to land a Great White.

The main images I have of cats on a leash are from cartoons of my youth. You would see an animated snooty cat attached by a leash to an equally snooty owner. All very buttoned down and repressed, so prim and proper that you could almost see the creases in the cat's fur to match the creases in its owner's suit pants. (It was meant to be funny, and in the context of the cartoon it probably was; i.e. pets look like their owners.) But it all reminds me of when as a teenager we were finally allowed to wear jeans to school instead of dress pants, and my mother starched creases into my Levis. (I was so-o-o embarrassed to wear those pants.)

I will have to admit that I saw a cat on a leash once that didn't seem to mind its situation.

It was at a party on campus. A very hippie chic girl with long blonde hair and a rawhide vest came in the room. She had on faded denim jeans with flowers appliquéd on them above her sandals. In the crook of her arm was this little short tail blue eyed gray tabby kitten. Around the kitten's neck she had loosely tied a long string of red fuzzy yarn as a leash. When she sat on the floor, she put the kitten down and it immediately started playing with the yarn. It didn't think the yarn was a leash; the kitten was too busy playing with the yarn as a toy. At that time of my life, I was a lot mellower about the whole leash thing. (I was extremely mellow in any circumstance at that moment.) And to be honest, I was more distracted by the girl's breasts playing peek-a-boo behind the vest than I was about the kitten's confinement by a piece of yarn.

Still, I have to say that denim jeans were never meant to have creases anymore than cats should be expected to use a leash.

You, or my cat.

You think it would be easy, but there are times this is not an easy choice.

Your girlfriend/boyfriend (it had better not be your spouse or you have waited *way-y-y* too long, my friend), or your cat.

There are many reasons for this to have reached this point.

First, you … are … an … idiot.
If you couldn't figure out that there were *issues* between your cat and the girl/boy you are dating right on the first night that they meet, you are an idiot.
A dunderhead.
A man/woman with a head of stone.
This should have been real easy to sense. Like when your cat is hissing, its whole body pulled back at an angle and it's taking swipes with claws bared in the air towards your visitor in its best imitation of *Wolverine*. Subtle things like that.

Secondly, the beer goggles were firmly in place (but your brain was rattling around like a pea in a gourd).
Still, no amount of beer, or wine, or booze (well, maybe tequila) should stunt your senses so much that you are ignoring your cat (who's probably your best friend) at this particular moment.

Thirdly, Mr. Idiot Jr. is doing a happy dance in your pants. If you cared to notice (and you obviously don't care), Junior has got its beer goggles on too. It's even pointing to them if you would just look.

Okay, maybe for some ungodly reason you missed the clues on that first night. (I know she/he was gorgeous. Blah, blah. Blah. Save it for the misery loves company session when you rehash all of this with your buddies/girlfriends over beers/wine.) There were clues later on that you just shouldn't have missed.

You've been dating a while.
Your cat isn't hissing anymore. (Good sign.)
But she is crouched under the chair as you and your new friend are making kissyface on the love seat while the TV is being ignored. (Bad sign.)
She has retreated far enough that you would only see her glowing green eyes if you cared to look. (Real bad sign.)

In fact, your cat has made a fist of one paw and is smacking it into her other paw like a ball player and his glove. (Impossible, but *if* she is capable of doing this; just run like hell out of the room.)

Or, if you are still stupid enough (or masochistic enough), to continue dating this person; your cat will usually give you a real blatant sign.

The lovemaking is over. The cat has been watching. Your date says she/he "Has to wash her hair before work tomorrow. Has an early meeting and is looking for her/his clothes." She/he finds them, is picking up their thong/thong and notices it is sopping wet.

Yes, kitty has left her final message. She has peed on your date's underwear.

Don't worry. At this point, whether it is "You, or my cat." has been decided for you.

Cats and the written word.

What is it with cats and the written word?

When I was a kid, our cat Princess would invariably climb up in my father's lap when he was trying to read his evening paper. Dad was not a cat person. Hell, he was barely a person person. (Long story. Years of therapy.)

Then when I was out on my own, the same thing would happen to me. I'm reading the Sunday paper (comics first or as I called them, "The College Section") and Krysla tries to worm her way onto my lap. If I'm reading a book: same thing. If I'm watching TV: not so much. And that's when I actually wouldn't have minded having her in my lap to pet. (Typical cat behavior: very cat-centric.)

When I was in college and working on a paper at the borrowed typewriter of my girlfriend; her cat would be there, trying to get in the way. When I got Krysla and we had a place of our own, it was even worse.

Krysla would hear the "clack – clack – clack" (one finger typist) and she would bound into the room like Superman ready to do battle with this clacking beast. She would try to lie on top of the typewriter, but I had this little Smith Corona and she oozed off the sides. So she took to sitting on her haunches beside the typewriter and would put just the front half of her body on it. This put her in position to take swipes at the letter arms as they rose out of the carriage.

She quickly learned that though they were small, those letter arms could hurt, and I learned to type even slower.

She would try to catch the arm by batting at it with one paw and usually end up with her paw stuck between the arm and the paper roller. Meowing in anger (because the metal demon wouldn't let go), she would hiss at it and me as I tried to free her paw. Then she tried to bite the arm. I put a stop to that quickly as I imagined the cost of dental work on a cat. (Plus with her, it would have quickly degenerated into a scene out of the dentist's office in "*Little Shop of Horrors*".)

I didn't have Krysla when I lived out west and switched from typewriters to word processors then to computers. She stayed in Ohio with a friend. The vet said she was probably too old to move and adjust to a new climate. By the time I moved back to Ohio after ten years in the desert, Krysla had passed. The apartment where I lived then didn't allow cats at first, then they did, but I just wasn't up to starting a new relationship.

Back to cats and the written word. The idea of cats interfering with someone's reading or writing has become so mainstream that it now appears in advertising. It's been around so long that Plato talked of Egyptians having to push their cats out of the way as they chiseled the hieroglyphs at Luxor (and then the cat would just go and lay on the papyrus rolls instead).

I don't think cats are actually attracted to the written word any more than they watch just certain TV shows. What they are concerned about is that you are paying way-y-y too much attention to something other than them. In a cat's world there is the cat, you, and a big blur of everything else punctuated by little sparks representing food, sex and shelter. Nothing else should exist as far as they are concerned.

It is the sun centric view of the solar system with a big ginger cat as the sun. (The Egyptians would have appreciated this view.)

Cats and Dr. Who.

I'm not a true Whovian that watches the show religiously and goes to conventions, but I do enjoy it and have watched Dr. Who on and off since the Seventies.

In the series, Dr. Who (a Time Lord that travels thru time and space with various companions) and his current companion Rose visit the planet New New York a million years in the future. There is a race of cats (the "Sisters of Plentitude") that had evolved over time and are now the nurses and doctors taking care of the humans of that planet. I thought this was so cool. I have my views on the human and cat relationship as it pertains to helping each other, and this fits into my long term views of that relationship. There had been an earlier show (a couple decades earlier – Dr. Who has been around forty years or more), where there was another race of catlike creatures called the Cat People. These are different from the show I'm discussing.

There are cats today that have extra digits on their paws and one of these could easily become an opposing digit – a thumb, which would be required to hold a pencil and attend college. It could be said that some cats are already smarter than some of their "owners" so what is to say that in a million years or so they couldn't have evolved and become doctors. (It takes almost that long today to become a doctor.) I have always felt that my cats could sense when I wasn't well.

I find it interesting that in this episode, not only is a cat race now the doctors and nurses, but they are also portrayed as being a bit nasty. They are using humans as breeders of various diseases so that they can then cure the humans of these diseases when needed. I would like to think that cats aren't quite this Machiavellian.

In the end, one of the cat race nurses decides to help the Doctor, and they expose the whole nastiness to the proper authorities and everything gets put right.

I just thought it interesting that a TV producer would have also decided that cats were empathetic and would make good doctors.

Black cats and bad luck

Black cats are said to bring bad luck. I think the bad luck is what usually befalls the cat. Some Animal Shelters will not let a person adopt a black cat in October because there are bastards out there that are sick enough to torture and/or kill black cats around Halloween? I'm sorry, but that's just sick.

All thru the Middle Ages cats (especially black cats) were persecuted by religious individuals and groups because they were said to be connected with witches and things that were evil. Cats are nocturnal and supposedly witches were out at night too. In some parts of Europe during those dark days, cats and witches were considered interchangeable with one being able to become the other.

I find it ironic that if people had promoted the growth of the cat population (instead of burning them); the Bubonic Plague might have been around for a shorter period of time. After all, cats would have killed the rats and mice that carried the fleas that were infected with the Plague. Instead, about one-third of the human population in Europe died from the Plague (and their own stupidity).

There are lots of myths about black cats, and not all of them say black cats are bad.

In most of Asia and the United Kingdom, black cats are considered lucky. There is a Scottish saying that a strange black cat on your porch will bring you good fortune.

In the US, black cats crossing your path are bad luck, but a white cat crossing your path brings good luck.

And the list goes on. It seems to depend on what part of the world and in what century you lived in whether a black cat was bad luck or good luck.

I personally feel that a lot of the bad rap a black cat gets is simply because the cat is black and can't be seen very well (If at all.) at night. This leads to the cat "suddenly" appearing in front of you, and thereby startling you. Humans don't like to be startled by anything; perhaps because of our "fight or flight" survival instinct. (If something suddenly appears, it may have been hunting you and you need to run away.)

During the Middle Ages most of the population of Europe couldn't read or write, and was basically ignorant. It was easier to just blame something for any misfortune you might have rather than trying to actually figure out what really happened. If there was an unmarried older woman that lived alone and had cats, she was suspect. If she knew how to use herbs to heal, that was good; but then maybe she knew herbs that would harm people too and that was bad. Because she had a cat for company, (and was smart enough to see that the cat ate the mice that were trying to eat her grain) then both she and the cat were suspect. It was a matter of ignorance mixed with jealousy and superstition. Put that in a pot and stir well, and you have a lot of myths and bad information.

Black cats were bad luck simply because they got bad press (and humans like to blame anything other than themselves for their own bad luck).

Other cats in science fiction.

Beware. They're everywhere.

It seems like cats show up everywhere; in print, on TV, in movies and on all sorts of cable and other media. I'm going to stay with Science Fiction since I have already touched base on it with Dr. Who, and these two show the opposite ends of how we think about cats.

The Kzin, or more specifically, the "*Man-Kzin Wars*", was a series of short story collections that I first read in the Seventies. It was originally written by Larry Niven and then taken up by several other writers with his blessings. It is still being written today. He basically created a universe where the human race battled a race of military cat beasts called the Kzin. These cats were bigger and meaner than any human and were out to dominate their part of the universe. They were ruthless fighting machines and had almost total contempt for the weak human race.

Basically if you took every hunting and fighting trait that a cat, especially the big cats (lions, tigers, etc.) had and made them that much stronger and more cunning, you would have the Kzin. They were flat out nasty and the humans usually only won because the Kzin were predictable in their actions.

This examined the worst attributes (from the human perspective) of cats. They were fearless hunters and we were basically just another prey. Put the average modern man on the African savannah today and we might find a few leftover pieces of him tomorrow. People forget and think that missus lioness over there is just a big version of the furball they have at home. Even trained zookeepers make a mistake and let their guard down and they die because of it.

At the opposite end of cat behavior is the character of "*Cat*" in the BBC TV series *Red Dwarf.*

This is a sci-fi comedy series that follows a guy on the space mining ship *Red Dwarf* who is frozen and wakes up three million years later. One of the beings he runs into is a descendent of a cat that he smuggled on board before he was frozen. He calls this character "Cat". Cat is played by a human with only the slightest of cat like physical attributes. (Such as; he grooms himself by licking the palm of his hand and then slicking his hair down.) In the sequence where we meet Cat, he is walking along wearing clothes that would suggest an extremely vain personality. As he walks, he is spraying things that he likes with a can of scent. Every time he sprays something, he says "Mine." He discovers the unconscious form of the lead actor and after a moment, sprays him, says "Mine." and walks on.

This is showing what a vain and pretentious creature a cat can be.

Both of these take a certain set of cat attributes and take them to an extreme; one for excitement and even horror, the other for comedy. And a cat is most certainly both. He can cause you to be excited with his actions, and ten minutes later you can laugh at his behavior. It's the yin and yang of kittydom. It's what makes a cat, a cat. We empathize with a cat's behavior as a reflection of our own. They seem to understand us, and we try our damnedest to understand them.

As it's been said before; women are from Venus, men are from Uranus, and cats are from a yet undiscovered planet past Pluto.

Now I know what a loaf of bread feels like.

Cats are kneady animals. In an alternate universe, they are probably the bakers.

If you watch cats when they are kittens nursing at their Momma's 24 hour milk bar, you will see them kneading their mother. I understand that it is an instinctive movement by the kitten to stimulate its mother's lactation. It's also a sign of contentment in the cat.

I heard it called "pawdling" when I was younger, and that's the term I usually use. Here in the South I've heard it referred to as "biscuit making".

The best example, and a classic, is the Saturday morning cartoon of the kitten and the bulldog. At the end of the cartoon, the kitten is standing on the bulldog's back, pawdling him. Each time its little paw goes down and scrunches the dog's fur, and then as it lifts the dog's fur, the fur clings to the kittens claws, then it lets go. Each time a paw meets fur, the bulldog makes an "ouch" noise, thru all the different variations you can think of for "ouch". It brings tears to my eyes because I've been in a similar situation where a cat is pawdling me. It's a pleasant cat torture that you get used to if you have cats with claws.

Josey will pawdle me occasionally when she is in an especially good mood.

Or better yet, when she had been out all night and I have slept in, so now her breakfast is horribly late (more than five minutes late in a cat's mind). Then after she's been fed, and when she is done with her after meal grooming and I've returned to bed to finish my sleep, she will, as Poe said, "Come a rapping, gently tapping, tapping on my chamber door." After pushing the door aside with her head (I always leave it open a little bit because I know she will follow in her own good time). She will jump up in bed and usually stride right over to her favorite après cuisine spot: my left armpit.

This means crossing over me.

If she's feeling spritely, she will just leap over me like a mare in a steeplechase clearing the lowest hurdle. Otherwise, she just walks on top of me like I'm a speed bump and nothing more. Why the left armpit is her favorite, I just don't know. The right one is closer. Whatever the reason, she likes the left one.

She usually just settles in, finding a curled position that's comfortable for her and allows me the best head rubbing access. (She will actually get up after I have started rubbing her head. Change position slightly, and resettle in a microscopically different pose, so that I can better rub the spot she has designated as this moment's target.)

But sometimes, and I truly don't know what makes the difference, she will decide I deserve a good pawdling first.

She has a light touch to her kneading: almost hesitant. Like a masseuse using feathers instead of the point of her elbow, she lightly pawdles away. But she doesn't have the endurance; she's a sprinter not a marathoner. And just as suddenly as it started, she quits and settles into her normal armpit routine.

Bubba Kitty was a power pawdler. He put his (ample) weight behind it. You knew you were being pawdled when he was at it. And he purred as loud as he wanted, letting everyone in the area know, "Yeah. It's me. I'm pawdling here." It could be pleasant, or funny, or kind of weird depending on what body part he chose for his ministrations.

Krysla was a pawdler extraordinaire.

She loved to do it to me on my stomach. When I was skinny, she did it there, and when I plumped up like the Christmas goose, it was still her favorite place. A girlfriend during this time period said Krysla was just sizing me up to see when I was right to be cooked.

Whatever the reason, I liked it when Krysla pawdled me. I took it as it was intended; a sign of contentment and I hope, of affection.

As I said before, she was a great cat.

Night patrol.

Cats are diurnal animals (animals that are active mostly at night) It comes out of their ancestry of descending from the Near Eastern Wildcat.

But why does it have to be such a pain in the ass for us?

Just because someone likes to go out and party all night (we've all had *that* roommate) why does it have to screw up everyone else's night? I mean, cats and humans have adjusted to having each other around, so why couldn't Mr. Meow change just a little more and stay in once and a while?

Because it's built into their DNA or some biological clock they have.

Millennia have passed as they went about their business at night. They have been designed by nature to hunt at night, so they are not about to change now. Your cat *wants* to be up and about in the nighttime. So your tabby wakes you up when she goes on her nightly patrol, or at least Josey does. Since she sleeps on my bed, I usually feel when she gets up and jumps off the bed. (I'm a light sleeper.) Normally, I just roll over and go back to sleep, but some nights her launching herself from the corner of the mattress is enough to actually wake me up.

Rather than just lie there, I get up and go to the bathroom. (Wonderful things happen to your plumbing as you age.) I can hear her back claws on the downstairs hallway parquet. (Make a note to trim those.) Then she's in the kitchen. She opens and closes cabinets looking for something to nibble on. (I may not be *completely* awake at this point.) Nothing new since this afternoon, so she's off to patrol the downstairs.

Having been up late a few times myself, I know her patrol route. She goes from room to room looking out windows, sniffing around every door for scents other than her own. She will jump up and check out the sofas and chairs just in case she needs a nap at some point during these exhausting surveillance maneuvers. In the kitchen, she gets up on her hind legs so she can push the trash can lid open with her head and have a whiff there. There are just last night's leftovers and some junk mail that's not worth going thru. Then she's off to the downstairs bath. She will sniff around the floor and then jump up on the vanity to check out the amazing looking cat that lives in the mirror. (Why do you think it's called a vanity?) If the first floor bathroom's door is closed, she will just spend extra time in front of the mirror in my upstairs' bath. (There is another cat in that mirror that looks amazing too.) Done with the downstairs, she will check her magic bowl and see if any food has reappeared since dinner. If not, she may come back upstairs, or she may decide the steps aren't worth the climb and settle for the couch.

If I had gotten up, I am back in bed and hopefully back asleep by now. Depending how she feels, Josey may just come back to bed, take a few sniffs of me in passing and go back to her spot for a well deserved nap. However, some nights (okay, most nights) she decides since the inside of the house is so damn boring, all the action must be going on outside. And that's when she really becomes a pain in the ass.

Sometimes, she just wants to be let out. She will run around on the bed and make herself obnoxious until I am awake. Then she will go to the door and wait there for me to follow. I give up at that point and just follow her downstairs. She will check her bowl and then go to the door. Some nights, it's zip, she's out the door. Other nights, she has to do this big song and dance of sniffing and looking out the open door etc. Whatever, she eventually goes out if the weather isn't bad.

You may ask why don't I just throw the cat out after dinner and not let her in till morning. If the weather is nice, I do. (Okay, yes. I'm a big softy.) In the warmer seasons, I have no problem letting her rampage thru the neighborhood at night. Otherwise, I like her company in the evening when she and I watch TV. I like the nighttime ritual of going to bed with me rubbing her head and she having an armpit nap before she moves to her towel for the serious sleeping. I like the fact that someone still needs me for something.

Maybe that's why I became her bitch.

Yakity cats.

It's 5AM and right now Josey is walking around outside meowing to her heart's content.

I know she wants in, but I want her to stay outside for a while. It's nice out. Even at 58 degrees (she is wearing a fur coat after all), it's comfortable. She's been inside too much lately and her belly is getting lower to the ground. (For a cat that never had kittens, she is definitely sagging.) So if she stays out, she will get bored with the back door and run around to the front door. I won't answer that either. She needs the exercise. I went for a walk last night after dinner; she went up and plopped down on my bed after her dinner. (I understand that Sumo wrestlers purposefully gain weight by eating a big meal, then immediately taking a nap.) This morning, she groomed herself and then reluctantly went outside after breakfast to water the shrubs. That took all of one minute and then she was sitting on the deck railing waiting on the doorman. (Me.)

She's moved off now. I can hear her meows fading a bit, so she must be over next door serenading them. They have a cat that looks a lot like Josey (could even be a litter mate if I didn't know better) and he is always walking around doing his "Meow ...meow." thing in the evening. Just talking to himself, I think, as he strolls around looking for his lost marbles.

So why do cats verbalize?

I was watching a show about cats on TV and the talking head said that cats have about 25 verbalizations that they use to talk among themselves, but there is only one set of sounds that they use exclusively with humans. That is a sort of meow/growl like "mer-rowl". And because humans live in noisy environments (to a cat's ears), they tend to say this vocalization relatively loudly to get our attention.

But obviously the number one reason cats vocalize is to get your attention and then remind you about the empty state of their magic bowl; a quick verbal rap on your knuckles. Then if you're lucky, she will meow/growl a mumbled thank you as she is gorging herself on crunchies and pâté. (But that caused some food to fall out of her mouth, so now she won't say anything else until she is finished.)

Food first. Plenty of time to talk later.

The number two reason is to get your attention for a specific reason. (Hey, look at me when I'm talking.)

The number three reason is to get your attention just for the hell of it. (Just reminding you she is there.)

The number four reason is that she is airing the dirty laundry about you and your family to all the neighborhood cats. (They are *such* gossips.)

However, Siamese are still the kings of the cats that verbalize a lot. (Yakity cats.)

I think Siamese talk so much because that is their version of radar. Bats use very high frequency sounds to bounce off their surroundings and get a mental map of what is around them. Siamese just yak their heads off and do the same thing. There is no other reason in my mind for why they talk so much. In fact, you had better like almost constant meowing if you're planning on getting a Siamese. They will *not* shut up. I've even seen them meowing non-stop as they eat. (I had a girlfriend like that. She talked thru everything, and I mean *everything.* It was a doomed relationship from the start.)

Yakity cats. To have one, you must *really* love one.

(Buy noise canceling headphones.)

Remember – "Meow" is a cat's "aloha"; it can mean lots of things.

My cat thinks it's a cow (and a dog).

The other day, Josey was out back in the yard doing her imitation of a cow.

She was eating grass.

I've been told that cats will sometimes eat grass to calm their stomachs or to help them throw up. I had friends in college that ate grass, (preferably in brownies) but for entirely different reasons. (It did seem to calm them down substantially.) It has to do with the chlorophyll or something (I told you I am not a doctor) in the grass helping sooth an upset stomach. I guess trying to hawk up a furball the size of a lime could upset your tummy.

Oh course, you could just stop licking yourself, and swallowing your own fur in the process. Remember the old saying, "Fur in, fur out." Yeah, like cats are going to stop grooming themselves, rather than put up with the occasional regurgitated toupee.

So, I guess I'm going to have to put up with hearing a "moo" instead of a "meow" out of Josey once in a while.

Then there is the other great piece of strange behavior in cats; when cats start imitating a dog.

Or the cat who drinks out of the toilet.

I have never had a cat that I have caught doing this. However, I have been at a friends' houses many times and I hear that distinctive "Lap, lap, slurp" coming from the bathroom. I am always relieved to see my friend's dog, (and not my friend) coming out of the bathroom afterwards. The dog will even be licking his snout with relish wanting to get every last drop of that wonderful liquid he just had. However, I have never been at a friend's house and seen a cat coming from the bathroom licking his whiskers with glee.

To me, dogs are basically disgusting in their habits, so drinking from a toilet comes as no surprise. But why would any gentrified kitty want to take a slurp? I can see a cat sitting around and having a nice cup of tea mid-afternoon with its friends (pinky claws held daintily outward), but all of them gathering around the toilet like pigs at the trough, having a good ol' slurp? It just doesn't make sense.

Again, I have been told (and again, I am not a doctor), that dogs drink from the toilet when they have decided that the water in their bowl is not fresh enough. *Toilet water is fresher?* Well, I guess you have to consider that every time you flush the toilet, the water is replaced and therefore is *fresh*. Still, I would think that there would be enough leftover germs that would cause even a dog (this *is* an animal that sniffs butts to get reacquainted), to reconsider having a good slurp.

But a cat?

I guess I will have to accept that other cats may have to get a drink from the porcelain throne when their irresponsible owners don't replace their water every day. (Hint. Hint.) However, I know Josey gets fresh water with every meal.

It's in the contract she made me sign. She likes a lemon slice and an ice cube in her water bowl on really hot days.

(I told you I was her bitch.)

No more tinsel on the Christmas tree.

I remember the Christmas that Krysla gave me an extra special present.

We were in the house that we shared in my hometown. I had finally decided to put up a small Christmas tree (or Hanukah bush as I would say to my friend Deb) in the living room. We had 11 foot ceilings on the first floor, so I could have put something in that rivaled the Rockefeller Plaza tree, but I didn't want it to be too flashy. So I just got a seven or eight foot pine. The kind that everyone normally gets.

It took me a couple days but I got it set up. (I am not the speediest person when doing stuff like this.) I had hot water radiators in that house and it seemed like they were on every wall. I wanted to make sure I didn't end up with a pine torch so I put an oversized water pan on the tree. You see, I have a black thumb; I can kill any plant you give me, so I figured the tree wouldn't last until New Years. I was only good at growing weeds. (Wink. Wink.) My brother Stuart had had the exceptional green thumb.

As I had no previous stash of trimmings, I bought some lights and bulbs. I'm sure there were the regular ornaments too. A garland and some tinsel would finish the tree. Had to have tinsel; a tree without tinsel at Christmas just wasn't a real Christmas tree. (I never understood why people would put tinsel on fake aluminum trees. Wasn't that redundant?)

Krysla had watched the erection and decoration of the tree with a mixture of interest and feigned indifference. She was somewhat leery of this new thing in the room, but she was also a cat. Curiosity won in the end. I was watching TV in the connected room and saw her approach the tree, sniff it and finally disappear under it. This was something I had worried about before I got the tree. In my youth our cat Princess had gotten up into our tree without anyone seeing her. Suddenly that tree started to wobble, and then over it went. Princess shot out of its branches like the proverbial bat out of hell. She spent the rest of that holiday growling at the tree whenever she passed it. So, I was justifiably worried about Krysla's intentions with this tree. After a few minutes, she sauntered out from under its branches with nothing more than a nip at some tinsel that blocked her way.

Days passed and the tree remained unmolested by Krysla. The three of us had actually made it to New Year's Eve without a catquake bringing down the tree. I had a few friends over for drinks and a nosh that night. Everything was going smoothly (considering everyone was drunk or numbed in their own chosen way), when Krysla moseyed her way thru the crowd. Krysla was ok with people around. I think she figured she could probably take down anyone in this crowd. Krysla was especially fond of walking across the glass coffee table like she was on a catwalk in Paris and it was the height of the season. (And here is Miss Krysla wearing nothing but a very tight fur by Au Naturel.)

Krysla was standing in the middle of the empty drink glasses, beer bottles and flickering candles on the table, when someone started to laugh and point at her. I looked at her and couldn't see what the fuss was about, then Krysla turned around quickly and I saw what was causing the commotion.

There was a piece of tinsel hanging from Krysla's butt with a clump of litter (and what the clumped litter contained) dangling from the end of the tinsel. Yes, it was Krysla's very special ornament; a dingle berry on a string.

Krysla may not have been mortified, but I sure as hell was.

I collected up my cat in my arms and proceeded to the kitchen. There, with the help of a paper napkin (In a very festive Christmas pattern.), I pulled on the dingle berry and watched the foil tinsel very slowly come out of her butt. That was the longest damn piece of tinsel I had ever seen. Krysla kept turning her head to see what was going on and gave a very indignant "Meow!" when I pulled the last bit out.

I set Krysla down on the floor and she proceeded to start cleaning herself. As I looked up, there was a girl standing in the doorway sipping on a drink. The girl looked at me and said, "Are you always so gentle with a...*cat*?" (Okay, she didn't say "cat".)

It turned out to be a very interesting New Year's Eve.

Watch out! (I don't know which one is you.)

In high school I knew this girl who had a Siamese cat for her pet.

There was nothing unusual about that. But you would expect an exotic cat like a Siamese to have an equally unusual name like Jasmine or Ming. Not this cat. If I remember correctly the cat's name was "B.T." which stood for "Bent Tail". This cat had a bent tail. I guess this is a common deformity (it's not anything hideous; just a tail that isn't straight) in Siamese. They also have another unusual defect; they have cross-eyes. Not every Siamese have these attributes, just the pure breeds. Undoubtedly from all the in-breeding required to make a pure breed.

What I find ironic is that all these so called Pure Breeds are in reality *mutants*.

That's something most people don't understand. And that is, to make a new "pure breed" animal, breeders have selected cats with certain attributes that they want to reinforce, and they interbreed these cats with other cats with the same qualities. This strengthens the wanted quality and after many generations you change a Near Eastern Desert cat into a Tabby, or a Long Hair, or a Siamese. (Dogs breeders did the same thing starting with the Wolf and getting everything from a Dachshund to a Great Dane.) Of course, modern breeders didn't actually start with the pure original breed; they started with what nature had already started mutating, a mixed breed descendant of the original.

So this girl had this adorable Siamese named B.T. that had one unusual behavior. It would run into things. Being cross-eyed, B.T. would see two images of what was in front of it and occasionally it would choose the wrong image as the real one. This happened when I met the cat. B.T. was playing in the yard and when the girl called him (it might have been a female; I don't remember), he ran across the yard and straight into a clothesline post. I mean it went *smack!* into the metal pole, shook it off and trotted over to the girl without any hesitation. I figure that the cat could smell which image of the girl was the right one.

This whole thing struck me as funny as hell. (I was seventeen and not very PC.) I'm sure that I said something like, "That had to have hurt." She just petted the cat and said that he was more cross-eyed than usual for a Siamese.

But this has made me think that we accept when our pets have some abnormal physical attribute (in this case the crossed eyes) probably better than we would if that same abnormality was in a human. Just think back to the playground in Elementary School and imagine how a child with crossed eyes would have been treated; probably a lot worse than any Siamese with the same affliction.

Kids can be cruel to other kids, but that same kid might surprise you with how they relate to a pet.

Thank you for being there for me.

It's winter. The wind is blowing outside, whistling loudly past your windows to get your attention and to remind you just how cold it is.

You are sitting on one end of the sofa, knees pulled up because the floor is cold (how can it be so cold in here when you're sweating like a pig on a spit on the Fourth of July?) even though you're wearing your boyfriend's/ husband's heavy hunting socks. You feel miserable. The snot machine is set up and running full blast in your left nostril. Your right nostril just whistles when you try to breathe thru it. The afghan alternates between being too hot and just scratchy. You've been watching the afternoon shows on TV but quit because they're all just *stupid*.

Did I say that you feel miserable? And you *really* could use a bath.

The teapot on the coffee table (is it still a coffee table if you have tea on it?) is empty under its normally cute bunny shaped pink cozy. And now that cozy just looks *stupid*. You really want another cup of tea, but don't have the energy to get up and make it. Maybe if you wish really hard, it will do it by itself. You scrunch your forehead with effort. Nope. That didn't work last time either.

Then, coming thru the gauzy vision you have because of the gunk stuck in the corners of your eyes, you see your cat walking (yes, walking on two legs) towards you. It has a fresh pot of tea on a silver tray that it's holding with its paws as it walks. There are some of the cookies with the mint flavored chocolate in the middle that you really like, and could have sworn you were out of, on the tray beside the tea pot. You can smell the wonderful aroma of your favorite tea that you are certain you had forgotten to buy last time you were at the store. Your cat comes to you and setting the tray down, starts to pour your tea for you. Then your cat says, "Mommy, can you get me a cookie? I can't reach it." And you realize it's all a fever induced dream; except for your kid standing there with a runny nose, a death grip on dolly and her blankey dragging behind her.

Crap.

Yep, you have one hellava fever. You force yourself upright and lead your daughter to the kitchen. You get your daughter and yourself a cookie, and then both of you trudge down the hall towards your bedroom. You don't even notice that your kitty is dutifully following you. Once you and the kid are snuggled in bed together, your cat jumps up and comes over to check on both of you. Then she settles down close by and keeps a half closed eye on you.

I've noticed over the years that my cats always know when I'm sick, or even just feeling poorly. Krysla was definitely that way. I would be lying in bed and Krysla would walk over and curl up beside me. I swear she would reach out and put one paw on top of my forearm and give me a look of, "We'll get thru this. Don't you worry." and Josey has started doing a pretty good job of it herself.

When I first moved to North Carolina, I had to adjust to a whole new set of pollens. For the first three months, I felt like crap. I thought about buying a breast milk pump to put over my nose to suck out all the snot. After Josey had relaxed around me and had started sleeping in my bed, I woke up especially miserable one morning. I really didn't want to get up or do anything. I was just lying there, trying to convince myself to get motivated.

Josey and I had already had our morning hello rubdown/armpit nap after I had gotten up to feed her earlier. She had wandered off to do a morning patrol of the house while I lay in bed accompanied by my misery. Suddenly she re-appeared on the bed. She paused to assess the situation, and then walked slowly but purposefully towards me. She tiptoed up and did her; "May I come aboard, Captain?" maneuvers. Then after settling in my armpit, she stretched her right paw and foreleg out so it went up beside my neck and then she laid her head flat against my upper chest near my throat. She adjusted her head and in the process rubbed her whiskers and muzzle against my neck. Then she lifted her head to look at me, gave me a "We'll be okay." look, then laid her head back down and gently purred away.

It just felt ... *nice*.

Cats and TV. Paws up or paws down?

Back in the Seventies, I remember being told to leave my TV on so that my cat would be entertained by it when Krysla was home alone. I also remember asking this person if there was any special show that I should have the TV tuned to for my cat; say a special on birds? This person actually told me that that would probably be the best choice. I felt like I was on *Candid Camera.* I believe I thought this was absolutely one of the dumbest things I had ever been told. I mean if I was going to leave the TV on for Krysla, I would want to leave it showing something that would improve her mind, like *Sesame Street* or *Pee Wee's Playhouse.*

I never saw Krysla watch TV. I mean *actually* watch it, as in sitting there and head moving back and forth with the action on the tube. Smoker on the other hand was an avid watcher. His head would move this way and that, and he would even give his own commentary to the actions in a series of varied meows. But finally, as with all of us, he would stand on all four paws and walk away, his tail erect in that exclamation mark pose that I think of as a cat's one finger salute.

I believe the thought behind this suggestion was that if the TV was left on, Krysla would hear the voices and think she wasn't alone. (Does anyone think *any* cat is that stupid?) Or if a nature show was on, she would be entertained by the birds and bright colors. (But what if the channel guide was wrong and she ended up watching an eight hour black and white special with sub-titles on French cinema?) Personally, I didn't want to leave my old TV left on at all unless someone was there with a fire extinguisher. So Krysla missed out on watching the birdies on TV.

As far as any of my cats were concerned, the TV was nothing more than a good place to sleep on a cold night. (It stayed warm for a couple hours after a full evening of being watched.)

Besides, TV was a vast wasteland for cats too. There were very few shows that had cats on as a character (other than Saturday morning cartoons) or even in walk-on roles as a character's pet. I think it was because cats were considered notoriously hard to train. (That's been disproved lately and you see more cats on TV today than 30 years ago.) Still, in the Seventies if a cat was on the TV it was either as a novelty act on the *Tonight Show* or a wild cat with *Jack Hanna.* Occasionally, you would see a cat in an actual TV show, but it would be as a disruptive agent. (Cat jumps on boyfriend at exactly the wrong time upsetting a romantic moment.)

Like *Rodney Dangerfield*, cats just got no respect.

Modern TV isn't much better. We still see cats in novelty acts on *The Tonight Show* and wild cats with *Jack Hanna*. There are a few regular shows that have cats as recurring characters, but again usually as a human character's pet. So, even though cats gave in and allowed themselves to be at least partially trained, they still have no major roles. (Except in Saturday morning cartoons where they have remained popular thru the continuous running of old cartoons.)

Just like so many other things, the cat's video presence has moved online, but that's a separate story.

Holy cats versus holy cows.

Let me delve into this for you.

I guess the first thing to dispel is that cows are not holy in Hinduism.

They are revered because they produce so many useful things – milk, curds, ghee (browned butter used in lamps), urine and dung (used as a fuel). So, the saying "Holy Cow" is actually very misleading, at least for Hinduism.

There were other religions that did worship the bull in the Mediterranean and in the Celt lands. But that was the bull, not the cow.

Cats, however, *were* worshipped in ancient Egypt.

The cat god Bastet evolved from a lioness-headed god and gave her name to the alabaster stone from which her statues were usually carved. She was worshipped from about 1,000 BC when domesticated cats were becoming popular in Egyptians homes. Bastet was usually represented as a cat-headed goddess with a woman's body. By the 5th century BC there was a temple dedicated to her in Egypt. There was an important and hugely attended festival in her honor every year which according to Greek historians consisted of heavy drinking by all participants. In Greek mythology, Bastet was also known as Ailouros. (Which means "cat" in Greek.) Eventually, the cat-headed goddess became just a cat statue usually of a black cat.

The Egyptian priests had taken the domesticated cat (which they honored because it killed mice and rats that ate the grain that was put in their charge by worshippers) and upgraded it into a god so that the common people would protect the cat for them. The more cats that were around meant there would be less vermin around. Since the priests were paid offerings in grain and were held responsible for the grain stores (which the priests held in trust for times of famine), the cats made them look good. At least the Egyptians priests gave the cats some credit by elevating them to gods.

If a household cat died in ancient Egypt it was common (if the family had the money) to have the cat embalmed or even mummified and buried in a cat cemetery. Families would even mourn for the deceased animal. In 1888, a farmer was plowing a field and discovered a plot with hundreds of thousands of buried cats in Beni Hasan.

Then we get to the Middle Ages in Europe, where depending on the country and the year, cats were considered evil and the companions of witches. So, cats have gone full circle from being worshipped as a god; to being burned with witches; to being the most common house pet in the world today.

I am quite happy that cats are just balls of fur purring away in our laps rather than gods that we would have to worship. (I would be too lazy to do the whole kneeling and worshipping bit.)

You think cats have an attitude now. Imagine what they would be like if we had to worship them.

Holy cats! No thanks.

The importance of the afternoon nap.

I have pretty much been an early riser during the last 30+ years of my adult working life. I learned to like to get my working day over with and on to my own time. My last stint as a cook/baker was in the beach city of Ventura, California. I went to work sometime between 2am and 4am and was usually done after lunch. I would walk home past the beaches with bikini clad girls playing volleyball in the sand (even on Christmas morning). It was a pretty good life. Go home after work, take a nap (I was exhausted by the work) then get up and go down to one of the beachfront restaurants or bars for a dinner/snack. Ten years of "work hard, play harder, die young". It *was* the eighties after all. I was in my thirties and dating nineteen year olds. My married friends back in Ohio hated me for it.

Almost everyone I knew working the last shift of the day either socialized or dated co-workers or people at other restaurants that worked that same shift. I called them "vampires" because if the job didn't drain you, partying till dawn did. They were mostly burned out by the time they hit forty. I didn't burn out, but my hands did; seven surgeries to correct damage in my hands, and they were still never right after that.

I had no cat then. Krysla had stayed back in Ohio with friends when I moved west. She was getting old and I didn't think she would survive the move. She died while I was gone.

I moved back to Ohio and ended up working in, then managing warehouses for the next nineteen years. I still got up at 4am, but I was rarely home before 6pm. It was hell. No bikini clad girls, no beaches, just snow every winter. The first three years of it I lived with a friend who had a family and a couple cats. That's when I got to know Bubba Kitty and V.D. (the cat, not the disease). Then I moved into my own apartment, and had a somewhat steady girlfriend who had two Labs. I didn't have a cat when I lived in the apartment, because I was never home. I would have needed two cats to entertain each other when I wasn't there. I just couldn't do that to the cats. It didn't work out with the girl, and I *know* it wouldn't have worked out with the dogs.

It didn't work out with the job either, I had destroyed most of what was left of my body with the years in the warehouses, and that's how I ended up with another set of friends in North Carolina and met Josey.

Not being able to work drove me nuts. I had started taking afternoon naps with Josey. About 2pm, she would wake up from her breakfast and want a cuddle to re-establish our social bond. I had learned the hard way that it was better to do this, than have her decide to have races around my bed at 2am to get my attention (and affection). Besides, I was tired by then from dealing with pain all day; the pills were wearing off and it was too soon to take more. A nap was more a necessity than an option.

I don't know whether I agree completely with societies that have afternoon siestas or naps or whatever you want to call them. Most people not in those societies consider this "slothful" behavior, even though scientific evidence points otherwise. But once I started taking afternoon naps with Josey, I began to see the benefit of these little naps. In fact, most of this book was thought up during my afternoon naps with Josey.

By "afternoon nap with Josey", I don't mean that she curled up against me and we bagged a couple hours of z-z-z's. She *did* curl up against me, and she *did* sleep for anywhere from 15 minutes to an hour. I, on the other hand, couldn't really sleep during this period; as I would have probably rolled over and had a very pissed off cat stuck halfway underneath me. I sorta dozed in and out of complete sleep. The warmth of Josey's body against me and the sound of her purring would relax me. That knot of pain in my lower back would begin to unwind. Finally, she would fall asleep and the purring would stop. She was out of it; oblivious to the world around her, knowing that I would protect her.

And during that time I would sometimes think about her and our relationship. (Other times I would think about how long it had been since I had my favorite pizza.)

At some point with a cat, the pet/owner thing becomes a relationship that's more than that. A friendship? Yes, but more: a companionship of some sort. You're both familiar with each other in that you know each other's habits, what pisses each other off, and where you enjoy being rubbed. The afternoon naps became important in that Josey and I would re-establish our connection with each other, and I would relax and reconnect with myself. And that last bit was more important than I had ever known. I can understand the afternoon siesta now.

And for Josey and me; I honestly think that Josey considers me that big dumb cat with lousy fur and horrible language skills that controls the magic bowls where food and water appear twice a day for her.

And I'm okay with that.

The purr-fect sound.

It's usually some sort of soft rumbling sound emanating from somewhere in the throat area. Whether it is coming from the larynx, or some special vibrating what-cha-ma-call-it; your cat is purring.

What does that noise really mean?

Some scientists believe that purring came about as the way for a mother cat and its kittens to find each other. It allows them a low volume sound that can only be heard at a close proximity to each other and not be heard by possible predators. Since a cat and its kitten both vibrate when they purr, it might even allow a kitten to follow the vibrations to its mother.

The most obvious thing it means is that the cat is "content." At least that is what I hear people say when I ask them. "My kitty is just content." Or happy. Or mellow. Or some other similar word.

But what exactly is your cat "content" about? It's last meal? How you are petting/rubbing/stroking/scratching her at that particular moment? What if you're not even touching her? Does a cat purr if there's no one in the house to hear it? I'm sure it has to be something simple; cats and dogs deal with the world at a very basic level. Maybe it has been passed down thru time as a way for a kitten to tell its mother, "I'm full and warm. You're doing a good job." And we're all just mother cat substitutes.

Josey has three distinct purrs:
1) The "I'm ok, you're ok." run of the mill purr.
2) The "You're petting me and I like it" purr.
3) And the, "Oh, my God, that's great" purr for when you hit the exactly right spot.

Number One is a soft purr that tends to lower my blood pressure (and if I don't watch it) put me to sleep. I've read articles in various magazines that cats (and some dogs) are especially good at de-stressing their owners. And I believe it; many times I've dozed off listening to that purr. This is the purr that Josey is doing when she falls asleep herself. She may be trying to de-stress me, but she got caught up in her own therapy.

Number Two is a little louder and varies in loudness and speed as you pet Josey. I think she is trying to give me instructions on what I am supposed to be doing to her. (Warm. Warmer. You're hot now.) It's ridiculous, but I will change how I am petting her, like switching from between her ears to under her chin, or just change up what I am doing in some way to get back to that steady constant tempo Number One purr. So if she's giving commands for what she wants; I'm trying the best I can to decipher them.

Number Three is the loudest; her whole body seems to shake when she does this one. This is the one she uses when she's just come in from the night. She's fluffed up (wearing her all puffed up fur coat) from the chill outside. She's dancing around me demanding attention and rubbing her face against my hands. As soon as I start to pet her, she starts up with Number Three. It's sort of a "pur-r-rump!" with the volume going up at the end. I get the feeling of her saying, "Yeah. Let's do this thing!" I have to almost laugh when she kicks into Number Three.

So, yeah, I think a cat purring (regardless of which purr) is the perfect noise.

It makes me feel happy inside. And I think she is happy too.

Please get done having the kittens. (This floor is hard and cold.)

When Krysla had her first litter, she had not had a Momma cat around to show her what there is to do during a pregnancy. So, as you probably have guessed, I became the Momma cat stand in. And in the immortal words of Butterfly McQueen, "I don't know nothin' 'bout birthin' no babies."

But I learned quickly.

Out of instinct, Krysla knew to find a hidden spot and build a nest. When she started disappearing into every nook and cranny of the turn of the century house that we shared, I knew that we were getting close. And I mean every nook and cranny. I ended up nailing the door to the attic shut. It was home to several bats (and supposedly one ghost of a former resident) I blocked off every hole that lead to who knows where in the basement. It was an old house with dirt floors in some of the basement that I was room by room cementing over. But the washer and dryer were down there, so I couldn't block it off completely like the attic.

Every time she tried to pull something together in some dank and dingy corner, I would take whatever she had decided the nest should be made from, and move it up into the bottom of the towel closet in my bathroom. Once I put a cat door in the bottom panel of the towel closet door, Krysla accepted the spot as okay security wise. Then, during the next week, I replaced everything she thought the nest should be made of, with old t-shirts and y-front briefs that I had kept around as cleaning and dusting cloths. Of course she had to rearrange them to suit her, but at least we had come to a compromise.

Things settled down to normal. (Or as near to normal as this situation could be.) Krysla stopped running around the house and settled back into our old routine of dinner, TV and then bedtime. Then one night, one miserable night of cold rain mixed with sleet rattling the windows, nature decided Krysla needed to learn her final lesson in birthing. Nature also decided it was time to teach me a lesson too. Sometime after midnight, Krysla woke me with a terrified look on her face. I truly mean terrified. I had never seen such a face on a cat. You could see the panic in her eyes.

As soon as she was assured that I was awake, she ran from the room leaving the water bed undulating in her wake. I got up and followed, bleary eyed and dragging my feet. She would disappear down the hall and scoot/slide around a corner. When she deemed I wasn't moving fast enough, she would return to hurry me along. She was running back and forth between me and the towel closet. I entered the bathroom to see her push the nest door open with her whole body as if she had decided the secrecy was over for now. She circled in the nest, looking at me in panic every time she came round to my view.

I decided this was probably going to be the night the kittens came. Since I don't drink coffee and needed caffeine, I got a can of cola from a mini fridge I had in the bathroom. (It was a big bathroom and I had essential supplies in the fridge for entertaining so I didn't have to go down stairs to the kitchen every time I needed something. So sue me; it was a *big* house.)

Krysla finally settled in the nest, but only when I was in sight. The tiled floor was hard and cold, so I went and got a couple blankets and my pillow and brought them to the bathroom. I made my own little nest. Krysla, of course, had to follow me while I was doing this. That became the dominant theme that night; I was never out of the cat's sight. Exhausted from waiting, I laid down on the floor and fell into fitful sleep. It was fitful because the only position I could be in that was acceptable to Krysla was that my hand had to be in the nest beside her head. That way she could smell my hand (with her cold wet nose to wake me up), lick my hand (with her raspy sharkskin tongue to wake me up) and finally bite my hand (with her sharp teeth) but never enough to hurt me, just to get my attention.

Finally she gave me quite a nip and let out a loud meow. Lying on my back, I opened one eye. We've all seen the scene on TV and in movies where the expectant and now imminent mother is crushing her husband's hand while giving birth. Krysla didn't have an opposable thumb to be able to grab my hand. But she had teeth. Sharp teeth. And they were all wrapped around my fingers. She held on tight thru the whole thing.

This was all new to Krysla and she was obviously scared by the experience. This was my first birth session too but I figured nature would just take its course. It did: seven or eight times during that night. And each time was a repeat of the previous one. After the last one slid out of her, and she was cleaning them (thank god, I wasn't looking forward to showing her how to do *that.*), I fell asleep on the cold hard floor.

My hand was still in the nest, now being assaulted by myriad tiny clawed feet as the little blind beasties looked for Momma. Momma licked my hand as well as her kittens.

All was as it should be: just one big family.

Sitting on the dock on the bay.

For most of the Eighties and into the Nineties I lived in Ventura California; south of Santa Barbara, north of L.A. and halfway to paradise.

From my apartment on the hill downtown by City Hall, I could see the Channel Islands and the beaches all the way to Oxnard. On the Fourth, I watched from my deck as the fireworks shot up into the sky above the bay. By day, those sparkling sandy beaches glistened with tan bodies year round. Girls (and guys, but who cared about the guys?) played volleyball in bikinis on the beach. A promenade, where people skated and strolled, walked and jogged, ran along the beach. Rock jetties jutted out into the water like outstretched gnarled fingers made of boulders and big chunks of broken concrete with rebar hairs.

I worked in several restaurants along that stretch of paradise over the years. My first job was right downtown by the hotel. And almost every morning, as the homeless slept in cardboard tents on the promenade's benches with newspapers over their faces, I would walk the five blocks from my apartment to the place where I was the morning cook/prep cook. It was before sunrise. It was eerily quiet except for the occasional car on the Pacific Coast Highway.

And I was followed by a gazillion wild cats; a veritable *herd* of mewing, hissing, tumbling over each other, furballs.

The tourists rarely saw the cats. I walked with my hand tucked inside my jacket holding one of my chef's knives. I don't know if I was more worried about an attack by a homeless guy, or having some enraged feline jump on me because my clothes smelled like food. *I* smelled like food. To the cats, I probably *was* food. If you have ever worked in a restaurant as a cook, you know you can't get the smell of food off you completely. You can shower, and launder your clothes every day, but your work shoes still smell like food. The cats know you have some relationship with food, and they want in on it.

Every once in a while I would walk along the promenade. One day I walked across the beach to one of the rock jetties. They were basically sand traps to keep the sand from moving too far along the beach as the waves came in and went out. I saw this older woman scrambling out on the jetty. She was stopping, bending down, and then standing and moving along the length of the jetty all the way to its end among the waves. I couldn't see what she was doing. The next day I mentioned it to one of the waitresses. She laughed and said it was one of the "Cat Ladies" who put food out for feral cats. I said she wasn't doing that good of a job because I walked thru a stampede of cats on the way to work every morning.

Another time, I saw the Cat Lady on a jetty and walked over to say hello. I was bored. She was there. It seemed like no big deal to at least say hello.

Boy was I wrong.

She watched me as I approached like I was certain to cause her harm. I was about fifty feet away and she yelled at me, asking "What do you want? I got my rights. I can feed these cats." And she went on this tirade like I was about to arrest her on some trumped up charge of disturbing the peace by feeding cats. I just waved and walked away.

On various days, I would see her, or one of the other women like her, feeding the cats. They all wore the same uniform of a floppy straw hat, sun glasses, a hoodie, Capri pants and sandals. They had shoulder bags (usually of macramé) which were stuffed with cans of cat food and small plastic containers that contained dry food. They would scramble across the boulders that made up the jetty like goats on a mountainside. I knew from walking on them that those boulders were dangerous; sharp edges and drift wood stuck out ready to cut you. They were slimy with seaweed and flotsam. It was hard to stay upright when you walked on them. There were also signs to keep off; you could break a leg etc. But the Cat Ladies persisted.

After about a year, I got a different job further down the coast in Oxnard and I didn't have time to watch the Cat Ladies anymore.

Every once in a while; I wonder if the Cat Ladies are still there, feeding the wild bunch. I would almost bet that the cats are still there.

This will be good for you. Honest.

Cats are like our kids in that we will lie to both of them to get them to do things they don't want to do. Such as go to the doctor. So why do we lie to our cats when *they don't understand English?*

I mean really now. Have we gone just a little bit over the edge when we feel it necessary to lie to our cats about taking them to the vets? I have actually sat in vets' waiting rooms with Krysla and listened to earnest pet owners telling their cats that:

> It won't hurt. (How does the pet owner know it won't?)
> This will be good for you. Honest. (You don't even know what the vet is going to do yet.)
> You'll feel so much better afterwards. (That's just hope on the owner's part.)
> I'll give you a treat afterwards. (It's not your kid at the dentist.)

You have to wonder what the conversations were like in the car on the way to the vets. Did the owner try to convince their cat that they were going somewhere else? By the sounds coming from some of the cars in the vet's parking lot, the cats didn't believe a word of it. You could hear at least one cat that is trying to dig its way thru the bottom of its carrier.

I feel sorry for the vet and his/her nurse. They know that they are about to be face to face with one pissed off cat most of the time. (Or one so sick that it doesn't care any more.) And one of the first things that they are going to do to Miss Precious is play hide and seek with a rectal thermometer. That has got to help the cat's mood.

It takes two of us when Josey needs her flea medicine. Since I live with two nurses, I let them apply the ointment to Josey's neck while I hold her. (Not that it takes a professional. I just think Josey would be calmer with me holding her.) But before we do this, we will discuss it in the other room in hushed voices. However, Josey always knows what's coming when she sees the two of us together. (Maybe we should spell out loud F-L-E-A ... M-E-D-I-C-I-N-E and that way she won't figure it out. I'm certain she can't spell.) It's not like we are giving her anything painful, just rubbing in the medicine on her skin.

But cats just *know* that you're up to something. It's part of the Kitty Defense System. The KDS is what allows cats to survive the curiosity factor and helps give them their nine lives. (I'm sure the Pentagon has DARPA working on something similar for the military.)

Since cats don't speak English (I know that comes as a surprise to many of you), they have developed over the 10,000 or so years that they have been around humans, the ability to decipher what we intend. Many animals that live, work or play in close contact with humans have developed this same sense to one degree or another. This ability to infer what our cats want by their meowing or actions is what allows us to have a relationship with the animal. If we didn't understand them in some way, we would never have become intertwined with them the way we are.

Through repetition of certain words, the cats have come to associate that word with some action that follows. We say "din din" and the cat knows food will appear in the magic bowl soon. Conversely, the cat will go and stand by its bowl when it's hungry and we will realize that and feed it. (Or like me, you'll say "It's too early. You're just being a pig.")

This is the way we *communicate* with our cats. All the other talking is just so much gibberish to Josey. I am not saying one or two word commands or questions that it can memorize and react to. Basically, I am talking to hear myself talk. We're the only two in the house, so I talk to her so I'm not lonely.

So when I say to Josey that "This will be good for you. Honest." I'm just trying to make myself feel better in the hope that I am not going to cause Josey any pain.

Yes, I did deserve a throne room. Thank you.

My housemates decided to get a canopy for the deck out back: a hexagonal tent thing with screened in sides. Nice. Keeps bugs out and gives us a place to have dinner out with nature. (But it is wisely separated from it.)

As you might have sensed, I don't enjoy camping. Lots of people do, I don't. I hated it when I was a boy scout in Ohio. It was tolerable during the spring thru fall seasons, but who wants to camp out in the winter? (Don't write me. I'm sure a lot of you do, but not me.) I was miserable. It was not the way I wanted to spend the week between Christmas and New Years. Being a Boy Scout was good for other reasons, and overall, I'm sure that I benefited from it. However, I like my creature comforts too much, especially in this time of my life.

It seems that Josey likes her creature comforts as well.

Not too long after we got it, I was in the kitchen late one night and I looked out across the deck. The canopy was up. The moon was almost full. The breeze rustled the screen panels making them sway like something out of the Arabian Nights. And there was Josey; sitting on her haunches in the middle of the glass table under the center of the canopy. I think she was waiting for Valentino to show up. She just needed a large perfume bottle ala "*I Dream of Genie*" on each side of her and the scene would have been perfect. Just like out of some silent movie.

In her mind, she must have decided that we had erected a throne room for her.

And she certainly deserved it: in her own mind.

That's the thing about cats; they seem to have a high opinion of themselves. I mean, the Pharaohs made gods of them, so I'm sure that inflated their egos a little bit. And the Egyptians even mummified them, which they didn't do to very many people, let alone many animals. So, I guess they had a few reasons to feel smug.

And a lot of people don't like cats for just that reason; because they seem haughty. I take that look on their faces to be a smirk, like they are in on some great cosmic joke; not that they prefer *Dijon* mustard on their crunchies.

So if Josey needs some shelter when the neighborhood Toms are worshiping her, then so be it. From sunrise to sunset, the canopy is ours; other than that, Josey can have her throne room.

I saw you swimming thru the grass.

Our lawn is always at various heights.

Different parts of it get mowed on different days; sometimes with the electric mower, other times with the string cutter. (It's my personal weapon of choice in the never-ending war on weeds.) Yes, I'm a weekend warrior in the nice lawn versus domestic jungle war. Occasionally, and I will admit out of sheer laziness (and an indifference to a set schedule), certain sections get a little long in the leaf. The front lawn is a delight (so the neighbors won't bitch) and the back lawn has a Little Vietnam section. It's almost wet enough back by the creek to have rice paddies and bamboo growing. Throw in a water buffalo and it would be a pastoral scene of just outside Saigon.

My house in Ohio was even worse. The front lawn almost didn't exist since the house was built within spitting distance of the sidewalk. (Something my neighbors there were well aware of, especially during watermelon season.) Neither side lawn existed because the lot had been subdivided for two other houses. And the back lawn ... well, the back lawn was just tall grass between an old carriage house and an alley.

I think it all comes from having to mow an acre of grass as a child with a push reel mower. You know the kind that you see people using in black and white movies. They're usually standing beside one mopping their brow with a handkerchief because you sweated a lot using one of those things. Sweat was actually the lubricant that made them run. (That's according to my neighbor's dad, "If you're not sweating, you're not using it right.")

Every once in a while Krysla would disappear in the house's backyard. I wouldn't actually see her, but I would see the wake she left in the tall grass as she moved through it. I think she thought that she was on safari; the great calico kitty following the well worn trails of the migrating chipmunks and wil-de-rabbits through the jungle grass. Then she would pause. She would rise up so I could just see the tips of her ears, then suddenly she would pop up in the air and pounce on some poor little vole or equally dangerous prey. That night she would be talking to the other neighborhood cats over cigars and port and admiring the newly mounted vole's head above the fireplace mantle. (Hey, that's the way she explained it to me. And I was not stoned at the time. Well, maybe a little buzzed.) All the while, I would be picking thistles out of her fur and telling her that yes she was a great hunter.

Josey on the other hand doesn't have that deep grass to hunt in or explore. In fact, I don't think Josey is that big on hunting at all. (Which is just shameful for a North Carolina kitty. She should have a gun rack above her litter box and a tiny jug of shine by her drinking bowl. However, I refuse to groom her fur into a mullet no matter how badly she wants it.)

No, Josey has other uses for her tall grass. She likes to go out and have a little chew of it every so often. (I'm glad she's picking up the habit of having some chew, so the neighborhood cats don't ostracize her. But I think she really does it as a breath freshener rather than a smoking substitute.)

And then there is the swimming.

Josey likes to swim in the tall grass. I will see her out back going back and forth in the grass like she's doing laps in a pool. I don't know what she's doing. (Maybe she's a little OCD.) But the best part is when she gets on her back and squiggles back and forth in the grass. It's probably to get bugs out of her fur where she can't reach with her claws or teeth. But I like to thin k it's something else.

There's nothing like getting to see your cat doing the backstroke in the high grass.

I'll let you know when you can stop.

I will be rubbing Josey on the head, and my hand will start hurting (an old injury), so I stop. Then the damndest thing will happen; she will push her head under my hand to give me a hint. If I don't take it, she even goes so far as to move her head back and forth like I'm actually rubbing her. (Actually this isn't a bad deal. She's doing all the work, but I'm getting the credit for it.) So I'll rub her head for a little while longer, and then stop again. Nope. Too soon. She'll push her head under my hand and start the process over again.

Because she's not done yet, and it doesn't stop till she's ready for it to stop.

Krysla was that way when we would be playing fetch. I might have started the game, but it ended when she was ready for it to end. Josey is that way only for the rubbing. She likes her rubdowns. (After all that sleep, she needs to stay flexible.)

She needs her "morning rubbing" after she wakes up and gets me awake. (I think she wants my hands to be flexible so I don't drop any of her crunchies.)

She needs her "mid-afternoon rubbing and armpit nap." (This is after she has slept eight hours.)

She needs her "after dinner, I've been outside and done my business, and now I'm back and I need some affection" rubdown and armpit nap.

And occasionally, she needs her "I've been outside for one last 10pm walk around", and I need a rubbing before I can sleep.

Each time, I will have to keep the rubbing going until she is satisfied. I have even developed a good arm across the chest to rub with the other hand technique. (Or the "affection backhand" as I call it.) Besides the push her head under my hand stimulus, she will just rub her cheeks a couple times against my hand. This is her way of saying, "You're family. We do things for family. I've done my part, now you do yours."

Again, I think this need for affection goes back to her almost wild start in life. Affection makes her feel safe. I can tell she feels safe because she lets her guards down a little. She closes her eyes tight. (No "slit eye", which I think is a little creepy.) You can just feel her *relax* as she stretches her front legs out like she's on a chaise lounge by the pool. (I'll have another capnip-tini, if you please.) She knows a good thing; and when you're enjoying something nice, you don't want it to stop.

I just wish she would leave a tip once in a while.

You are truly a slut kitty.

Cats can have kittens by multiple fathers in the same litter.

Krysla made this abundantly clear to me. I don't think any kittens that she had in any litter were true brother or sister; everybody was a half-sibling because none of the kittens in a selected litter looked anything like another one in that same litter. I figured this was just because Krysla was a massive slut in the cat world. Upon doing some research, I found that this was quite common in an urban setting. (I owe Krysla a posthumous apology for calling her a slut-kitty.)

My roommate and I would refer to Krysla's litters as the latest United Nations of Kittydom. Her litters were always so colorful; blacks, whites, gingers, tabbies, calicos and grays. She was a tortoise shell calico which is a blend of several shades of browns, oranges and black in a mottled pattern. She did have a pink nose that sort of stood out. I don't remember her having anything like a Siamese blend having snuck into one of the batches.

Let me give a quick explanation.

Cats have several mating seasons a year where they go into "heat" and can be impregnated. Cats, unlike humans, don't secret a mucus shield. This mucus plug is what normally prevents multiple fathers in humans. Though extremely rare, humans can have multiple father babies. (This is not the same thing as fraternal twins.) And cats are stimulated to release eggs by the withdrawal of the male cat, whereas humans release ovum as part of the monthly cycle. What all that means is that it is easy for cats to have multiple fathers.

One last interesting fact is that cats in urban settings are more likely to have multiple fathers, whereas cats in rural settings will have fewer fathers of a single litter. This is thought to be caused by cats in cities having more rivals available for breeding due to cat density. Cats on farms have fewer cats in any given area, so it is easier for one cat to stay near the mommy cat while she is in heat and take advantage of the situation.

Okay. I have put my cammo baseball cap back on.

So, if you look at your cat's next litter, and unless you've been controlling the studs for breeding purposes, don't be surprised by the mix of what is produced. And no, your cat's not a slut kitty either if it looks like every single kitten had a different father.

Pet cemeteries.

Not the kind that Stephen King writes about. I still can't hear the sound of a Velcro hook and eye style fastener being pulled apart without thinking about a cold dead cat body being lifted from the frozen ground. And yes, the separation of frozen corpse and ground does sound like that as I can personally attest. (Take a moment and get over the "yuck" factor.)

Do you have a pet buried somewhere in your backyard? And who hasn't flushed a pet fish down the toilet? (Those goldfish at county fairs should just be taken home and flushed because the likelihood of them surviving is probably close to nil.)

I have buried a few cats over the last forty years. It's something I probably won't really ever get over. I have always been really close with the cats in my life.

Krysla died chasing a squirrel or something across the street. She got hit by a car. She had been staying with my best friend in Ohio when I moved out west. (She would have been too old to travel and then adjust to a new climate.) Plus I ended up living with friends out there for a while until I got my own place. But my friend in Ohio called and told me about it and that he had buried her out in a flower bed alongside their back yard. I said that was good, she'd had good times in that back yard.

I know another individual that even made coffins for his dog and cat. He was a construction worker by trade and he felt they deserved something better than a shoebox for the cat and a trash bag for the dog. It's not that he was obsessive about his pets; he just felt they had been members of his family and they deserved what any family member would have gotten.

Most major cities in the US have pet cemeteries; actual outdoor cemeteries that are devoted to just pets. I believe Los Angeles has a large one where famous Hollywood animals are buried. Here locally, Greensboro has a pet funeral service but I don't know if there is a pet cemetery. Having a funeral for a pet and having a pet cemetery are two different things.

Burying a pet (especially a cat or dog where they might have lived in the house with you) is a personal thing. I think that is because house pets are considered your friend. They've been a companion who in many cases shared your bed, your couch and even your lap. You've talked to them like they understand you. (And in some cases you think they understand you better than some humans do.) You have fed them, groomed them, kept them warm and safe and taken them to the doctor when they have needed it. You have made sure they got their vaccines and took their pills when they were sick. You've worried about them when they didn't come home at night. (How many times have you secretly worried about getting a phone call in the morning from someone that has "found" them and you hold your breath until the person says they're all right?)

But that is part of what pet cemeteries are all about. For those that can afford it, and maybe went a little overboard while the pet was alive, a pet cemetery might seem justified.

I think that a nice grave with a little marker with the pet's name on it is enough. Maybe put it in that corner of the garden where she used to sun herself. Especially if you can see that spot from your kitchen window when you're cleaning up after the family dinner.

And then you can smile and remember when she...

How can you be comfortable with all that fur on?

It's 85 degrees out and I break out in a sweat just lifting a beer to my lips.

Josey is lying under the patio table licking her paws acting totally cool and collected.

I'm sitting here in just my cammo boxers. She's in a fitted fur coat. What the hell is going on here?

It's always amazed me how a cat seems to act like weather doesn't bother her. I mean, yeah, if it's 10 below outside, it's obviously going to affect her. She won't want to go out into the cold and if she was already outside, she's fluffed up to double her normal size. (This is the cat version of the puffy coat.) Then if it's 85 like today, she's acting all nonchalant about it. I look over at the neighbor's deck and their dog is panting like crazy. (Good. She brought a bowl of water out for the mutt and put it in the shade.)

I rarely see a cat panting and I don't understand if she can sweat how it would do any good thru that fur. So, I did some homework.

Sorry. I'm going to put my professor hat on again. (But I'm wearing it backwards.)

Most cats have two layers of fur; the undercoat and the guard hairs. (Some cats have three layers, but that's just to show off.) The undercoat is the soft fur closest to her body. That's the stuff that gets all over the couch and your girlfriend's sweater. It's also what the cat licks off and makes up those wonderful hairballs you see her hack up every so often. The guard hairs are the longer hairs that actually have most of the cat's color and pattern on them. (Interestingly, a tiger's stripes go all the way down to the skin which is also colored in a striped pattern.) Whiskers are also thick hairs but have nothing to do with a cat's temperature control. (If you want to know more, look it up online.)

Cats do sweat, which I didn't think they did. But like I thought, it doesn't do a lot of good thru their fur. They beat this in a couple of ways. First, they sweat thru their paws. Next time you take Miss Kitty to the vet and she's nervous about being there, look when the vet picks her up. There just may be four wet paw prints on the paper on his exam table. (I usually leave a wet butt print on my doctor's exam table.) Second, they beat the heat by licking their fur. Even though it's not touching their skin, the saliva evaporates like our sweat does and helps cool them that way. Third, they can pant if they really have to. But if your cat is panting, get it to a cooler spot and give it some cool water. If it doesn't stop panting soon, call your vet.

Also, it's not your cat's fur that your girlfriend is allergic to; it's her dander. When her saliva dries, some of the stuff in it becomes a flakey material and that's the dander. So your girlfriend isn't allergic to the fur; she's allergic to your cat's spit. So just have your cat quit spitting on your girlfriend. (Even if Miss Kitty is just expressing her opinion of your date.)

So, even though I was stripped down and sitting in my lounge chair (and having a beer) to cool off. Josey was sitting under the table which was shaded by the canopy. That way she could look cool and nonchalant in her fur coat in the heat. (My girlfriend says I have a fur coat too, but I just look like a mangy gorilla.)

How the hell did you get in there?

Cats get into the darnedest places.

This past fall, I heard Josey meowing plaintively about something. When I went to find her upstairs to see what the problem was, I couldn't find her. I walked in the hallway towards her meowing and then I would realize that it was coming from behind me. Turning around, I walked the other way and after I passed the bathroom, I realized that once again, her meowing was coming from behind me. But there was nothing in the hall but the laundry shaft in the wall. Feeling like an idiot, I looked down that. Nothing. (Honest. I only felt like a little idiot doing that.)

The only other opening was the door to my bathroom. I opened the towel cupboard and she wasn't in there. There really wasn't anywhere else she could be; after all, it was a bathroom. Then there was another meow. This one was at floor level.

My roommate had been fixing a leaking pipe in the bathroom. The work required that the vanity be partially disassembled to get at the pipe. The meowing got louder as I got closer to the vanity. (Like she was guiding me with "Warmer. Warmer. Hot!") Getting down on my hands and knees, I looked under the vanity, and was greeted by a loud and somewhat plaintive meow. Then a paw came out from between two boards. Josey had decided that this was a wonderful new area to explore and found that she could just squeeze past some wood and end up above the ceiling to the kitchen below the bathroom. Unfortunately, when she entered, the board slipped in place behind her. I immediately had thoughts of the Poe variety of Josey being walled up when the work was done. I got my roommate and he reached in and moved the board. Then with some coaxing, we got her to come out. I stuffed some towels into the opening until it could be permanently sealed.

The adventure with Josey reminded me of another search and rescue mission from twenty years ago. I was involved with a girl and was staying at her apartment for a while. I was home alone with her two cats while she went to work. Again, it was an episode of hearing one of her cats meowing and not being able to find it. When the girlfriend came home, we looked everywhere; even checking out a small ledge outside the windows that went around the exterior of the apartment building. The cat was nowhere to be found. Finally, we were sitting on the bed and we heard the faint meowing. I could see a light bulb go on above my girlfriend's head. She reached down and pulled out a drawer from under the bed. Inside, with her underwear, was her cat.

Both events made me think why the hell do cats get into all the weird places that they do?

Is it just natural curiosity? After all, we all know, "Curiosity killed the cat." I would think that a few thousand years of cats being overly curious (and killed for the effort), would have eliminated that evolutionary trait. Something that leads to extinction really shouldn't be a trait that gets passed on to future generations. But it has.

Think of all the weird ass places you've found your little furball of wonder. You find cats everywhere; in drawers, in cupboards, suitcases, car trunks and closets; under sofas, *in* sofas. (Yes, I had a cat that had torn a hole under a sofa and would crawl up into the upholstery.) It seems that if they can get their head in someplace, there is this urge to put the rest of their body in with it. And their body is built to do just that. Cat's shoulders are not locked into place like ours are; theirs float unattached to each other.

I think it goes way beyond just curiosity. Curiosity is just the first step; but then we have to ask, *why* are they curious? And I think this is where the survival instinct comes into the equation. They are always looking for that safe "hidey hole". Cats have survived because they always know of some safe places that they can just squeeze their bodies into and where something that is hunting them, can't reach.

So, that behavior of your cats that drives you nuts and causes you to ask, "How the hell did you get in there?" may be nothing more than one more survival instinct that has given cats the reputation for having nine lives.

And if nothing else, it may just drive their predators nuts; just like it does us.

Why did you tattoo my car with your paws?

You just spent hours washing and waxing your car. You go in for a cold one. When you come out, there is a track of dirty paw prints up across your hood, the windshield, across the roof, down the back window and over the trunk lid.

Why? Oh, dear god, why?

Damn it cat, couldn't you have gotten the wanderlust out of your system *before* I washed and waxed the car? No. You purposefully waited until I was completely done. I saw you pretending to be asleep under that bush, just biding your time. Your eyes just slits as you watched me busting my hump to get this done before the guys came over to watch the game. I should have known better. Now I have a paw-print racing stripe. Not even manly big ass tiger paw prints. Nope, just dainty little puddytat paw prints. And they aren't even in a straight line! You got distracted in the middle and wandered a bit.

Ah, the frustration. At least your wife thinks it's kind of cute. (Oh, that just made it worse didn't it?)

I can remember different male family members being if not enraged at least thoroughly pissed when they saw little paw prints on their previously clean cars. Even though the cat probably did it (though one night I saw a raccoon walk across my roommate's car), what can you do about it?

Yell?
Throw the bucket of wash water at the cat?
Try to spray the cat with the garden hose you were using? (And end up spraying your car instead.)
Curse a blue streak?
Go sit on the chaise lounge while you have another beer? (Got a show of hands for this one and I didn't even ask for it.)

In reality, there's not much you can do about it other than wash the offending paw prints off your car. Cats will instinctively go for the highest point they can reach in any given area. (The roof of your car is the high point in your driveway.) Domestic cats are basically sight hunters, so they will want to get as high as possible to check out what prey is in the area. (Those damn chipmunks are elusive as well as dangerous.) Then they will get down on the ground to stalk their prey. I have never seen a house cat pounce from above when hunting something. They might, but I've never seen one do it. I've seen them jump down from a perch and chase something, but that's not the same as jumping down and landing on their prey.

They will also go high to see if anything is stalking them. (Or to just irritate the crap out of the noisy Chihuahua next door.) Domestic cats like to find a high spot inside the house too. Such as the top of a bookcase etc. but that can be more of wanting to feel secure rather than hunting.

So, you're just going to have to put up with a paw print tattoo on your car every once in a while.

Just be thankful it wasn't a skunk that had decided to spray paint your car.

You did that trick before.
(Why won't you do it for my friends now?)

Some years ago, I remember seeing a show on TV about a guy that trained cats for his circus acts. He said that he didn't set out to train a cat to do a specific trick. He would watch the cat, find something that she did normally, and then figure a way to work that into his act.

I have talked about how Krysla used to play fetch, and Josey has her moments when I can get her to do a pirouette on her hind legs while I am dangling food over her head, (I'll do one too for a good rack of ribs) so it *is* possible to get your cat to do tricks. But why, especially when your little beastie has everything down pat, does she suddenly decide that she doesn't do that anymore when you want her to do it for guests?

It's not like I'm asking her to put on a show for the neighbor kids. We're not going to be Mickey Rooney and Judy Garland fixing up the barn and saving the orphanage. I'm just asking her to do for my friends. A simple little thing that she's done dozens of times for me. And it's not like I'm finicky. As long as she gets it close to what I told them she could do, (so I don't look like a complete idiot) I'll be happy.

Cats are known to be inscrutable and mysterious. But there should be a simple answer for this.

Let's see:

1) She knows how to do something cute/funny/clever.
2) It is something that is relatively easy to do. (I could probably do it.)
3) She has done it many times before and therefore shouldn't have any stage fright.
4) She likes to screw with my head.
5) She knows it pisses me off when she won't do it.
6) She knows I'm trying to use her trick to impress a new girlfriend.
7) She knows I hate being embarrassed.
8) She knows how to screw with my head and piss me off by not doing the trick to impress my new girlfriend and embarrass me in front of my guests.

That's it. Number eight.

The simple answer is that she is a cat.

Cats can do wonderful and amazing things. They can make you feel all warm and squishy inside. (Well, not me. I am immune to her catty wiles.) They can help lower your blood pressure. (Not in this example.) Cats provide company and companionship to people that live alone, or even people that live with other people and just feel alone.

But most of all, cats will be cats and every once in a while they seem to get a really good chuckle out of screwing with your head. It's in our original contract with them; I will keep vermin away for you (and have a nice meal in the process), but you have to let me dick with you every once in a while. (So I can keep this Mona Lisa smile on my face.)

Okay, it's worth it to see that smile. Where do I sign?

Using your cat as a dishwasher.

Using your cat as a dishwasher; or are you really that lazy?

It's probably not the best idea. I know guys that are constantly giving their empty (obviously not quite empty) dinner plates to their dogs so that the animals can "lick the plate clean". This is right after said dog has licked his genitals "clean". Yummy. This is not a good idea because cats and dogs can't eat certain human foods without dire consequences. Chocolate comes to mind for both dogs and cats; for humans – good: for the little beasties – bad. I've even seen guys put down plates that have leftover hot sauce from some wings, just to see if the dog will taste it. Really stupid idea buddy. Is it really that funny to see if you can make your pet sick on purpose? Which one of you is actually the "dumb animal?" (Sorry. Some things do make me get up on my soapbox.)

Luckily, Josey is not a big lick the human's plate clean sort of cat.

She does like to lick my ice cream bowl when I am done with it and nothing is left but some creamy residue. And occasionally I will give her some "finger food" (food bits that I have poised on my finger tip) such as cream cheese, or a bit of Swiss cheese, and especially a cheese puff end cap. But she doesn't get meat bones or any real food item. She does get a bit over zealous when she smells something left on my fingertips after I've been cooking. (Honest, I do wash my hands several times when I'm cooking and I use a hand sanitizer.) The other morning I had cooked some bacon and she went absolutely berserk trying to lick all the leftover grease off my forearms. (Note to self, wash forearms too when cooking.)

However, Krysla would eat leftovers.

She absolutely loved spaghetti and a mini meatball made especially for her. She would even eat the pasta. I think that was just because there was meat sauce on it. (Yes, I like a meat sauce *and* meatballs on my pasta. We are carnivores after all; meat makes the vegetables taste better.) And she would eat some table scraps like chicken and turkey, but she wouldn't beg for them. (However, she would jump up on the table if spaghetti was involved.) I had forgotten what a thing she had for spaghetti.

Again, I've been at people's houses when they give their cats some table scraps. But I insist on one rule; don't feed the cat scraps from your plate while you are still at the table with your guests. It's rude. You are equating what you just fed me with what your cat likes. In other words, I'm eating what you consider cat food.

I had a vet tell me that feeding your cat (and dogs) a lot of table scraps will make them snooty eaters and they may eventually not want to eat the prepared cat crunchies and pâtés. Then you are screwed. If you end up having to cook a meal for your cat every time, I'm sorry, but you're an idiot.

So, you can maybe use your cat as a dishwasher on a selective basis. Just don't get lazy about it. Prepared cat foods are manufactured to be good for your little beastie and complete in its dietary needs. Scraps are just that – scraps: bits and pieces that are leftover and unbalanced health wise.

Why can't you leave me alone for ten minutes?

She's always underfoot.
She's in your face when you try to read or watch TV.
She is constantly demanding attention.
So, why can't Miss Kitty leave you alone for ten minutes?

Because she lo-o-ooves you. (Ah-h-h.) Well maybe she does, but that's not my point.

Cats are social animals and need a certain amount of interaction every day. Today, for example, Josey has been throwing a snit and ignoring me because I made her stay out all last night. (Which was actually from midnight to 5am.) It wasn't so much that she was outside (it was 65 degrees out), but that it rained all night. She has several dry places outside where she can sit out anything short of a tornado or Hurricane Katrina. Well, last night was one of those nights when I really needed to get some sleep and she's been acting up at night because her new boyfriend has been hanging around outside calling her name. (She answers to any version of "Meow.") That I need my sleep is not something that I can explain to the little furball, and I thought, I'll just make it up to her tomorrow. Tomorrow came and I was running all day trying to get some very important errands done; things that absolutely had to get done today.

So, Josey built up a good snit and has been driving it around the house all day and running over my toes with it just so I know she's upset. (Snits are very good for this, especially the 2013 model which gets excellent mileage from just one period of neglect and they come in several nice colors.) She's really just been on my bed all day glaring at me when I dare enter my own bedroom. And it all boiled down to the simple fact that I just didn't have time for her today. Now, I have made up for it since dinner. She had two long armpit naps and I allowed her to steal a piece of Swiss cheese when I wasn't looking. (I just had to push it closer to her twice.) There have been some things building up in my life and now I really have to spend some time getting them straightened out and/or finished.

Meanwhile, Josey still needs her daily quota of love and affection, which I would normally go out of my way to give her. (I am her bitch after all.)

Tomorrow is Saturday and I have nothing planned other than watching Formula 1 racing on cable. I can do that and give Josey a good dose of affection in the morning. I have plans to swing by one of the big box pet stores later in the day and look for a toy that she might play with while I am busy or gone. If I can wear her out more during the day with loads of affection from me, she won't need me at night and will want to go out and play with the neighborhood cats and I can get my sleep. (Yeah! Win, win!)

She won't leave you alone for ten minutes because you haven't been giving her those ten minutes in a daily dose. It's easy to forget about a cat and her needs because they seem so damn independent. They are, to a certain degree. They will run on forever as long as you keep topping off their tank of affection. And it's not just loving the little beastie; it's the socializing (even if you are just sitting beside each other on the couch) and play time (you are simulating hunting with her) that matters too. Especially if you only have one cat and you're gone a lot.

All pets need some of your time. They are not decorations for your home; they are part of what makes a house a home.

Kitty, you can light my fire.

I can't remember if it was late fall or early winter (in northern Ohio, they blend together) but I know it was miserable out.

It was cold now and it had been raining earlier in the day. I had been out drinking with friends and had walked home from the bars. (This was easy to do because I only lived one street away from the main drag.) It was after midnight and I was going home alone. It had not been a great evening. As I put the key in the front door lock (with great difficulty, the lock kept moving), I saw Krysla come charging into the living room and slide to a stop on the other side of the entry door. She sat there looking at me wondering why it was taking me so long with the door. I explained to her as I fumbled with the lock. Anyone close enough to hear and see me would have wondered why I was talking to seemingly no one. (Anyone that really knew me would have known I was talking to a cat. I don't know which scenario was worse.)

Earlier that evening, I had left work when we closed the family store for the night and walked a few blocks to have dinner by myself. I was in the mood for a steak and didn't feel like going to a grocery store and then home etc. so I chose an eatery nearby where I knew the chef. They did a good porterhouse. I had that with the usual complement and some wine. Afterwards I wandered down to the bar downstairs. (This was the main reason I had come that way.) I usually had good luck in this bar on a Saturday night.

Maybe I was too early, or my mood showed that I wasn't really in the mood for company, whatever the reason I wasn't having any luck. I talked over drinks to a couple girls that I had known previously, but it seemed that none of us felt like having a repeat. First one girl wandered off, then the other. I had spent a few evenings with one of the bartenders, but when I talked to her, she said she was the closer that night. That would have meant no action till 3am and I wasn't going to be functional by that time of night. I bid adieu and walked my sorry ass home.

As I said, Krysla met me at the door. She always met me at the door. If I could have just trained her to open the door for me occasionally, it would've been a great help. But I finally made it inside. Krysla was making fast figure eights in her usual welcome home dance. I reached down, scratched her head quickly and she trotted off to the kitchen, her tail doing its own welcome home dance as she walked. (Her tail always did this question mark, exclamation mark, question mark, exclamation mark movement as she walked when she was happy.) I hung up my coat. I followed and gave her a few crunchies in her bowl as was our nighttime ritual.

I was exhausted from work and a less than satisfactory evening out. Going upstairs to my bedroom, Krysla zoomed past me and stood waiting at the top of the stairs. Again, I scratched her head as I reached the top of the stairs. I figured she would excuse me for not showering or brushing my teeth and I just headed straight to the bedroom. She beat me to my bed.

It was an old painted lady of a house that I was remodeling. In the front was a big hexagonal bedroom over the first floor front waiting room. My king sized waterbed took up a good portion of the room, but I liked my creature comforts. The three sides of the room facing the street had windows though I planned on closing over the middle one that was at the head of my bed. It leaked cold air in the winter, so come spring it was going to be gone.

Krysla was waiting on the spare pillow, which was hers when there wasn't company. When I climbed in and pulled the covers up, she immediately nestled herself against me. She yawned when I rubbed her head. Her breath smelled like crunchies. She had been sleeping, waiting for me to get home. I had come by about three in the afternoon and made her dinner. Like some old married couple, we quickly fell asleep.

The cat was jumping up and down on me. I was not happy. I looked at the clock with one eye. It was around 2:30 am. Not my usual wake up time. I knew Krysla couldn't be hungry, so I said "stupid cat" and rolled over to go back to sleep. She was on top of me again. As I started to sit up, Krysla ran over to the window and meowed like the world was coming to an end. Then she ran over and rubbed and licked my face like she had never done before. There was a weird light in the room, like one of those fake fireplaces gives off. Krysla was back in the window, meowing and looking at me. I swear she was scared.

I tumbled out of bed and walked to the window wiping the sleep out of my eyes. At the window, I looked out and saw that my neighbor across the street's garage was on fire. Grabbing the phone by the bed, I called 911 and reported what I saw. Someone else had already called it in and the fire engines were already rolling up my street as I hung up. I picked Krysla up and held her close as we watched for the next hour as the flames were put out. When we saw the neighbors in the street and they were ok, we went back to bed.

The next night, I watched Krysla enjoying the diced up prime rib I had brought her for dinner. It was the least I could do.

Your kitty has decided it doesn't like its food.

You and your cat have gotten into a nice groove when it comes to mealtime.

Your cat likes her crunchies with side of pâté. (I have to mix the pâté in with the crunchies or Josey will just eat the meat paste and leave the crunchies, then give me a look of "What happened to the smelly stuff? I want some smelly stuff too.", like she never got any.) You give your cat fresh water with each meal and you feed her at the same time ever day, which she knows because she is there waiting for you.

If she's really hungry, she'll do her happy food dance for you while she waits. You know the dance. Figure 8, rub your leg. Figure 8, rub your leg. Up on two feet, paw the air. Down and meow. Then repeat. (I can get Josey to do a pirouette while she's up on two legs by moving her bowl in a circle around her head. She follows the bowl.)

Then one day, it happens. You put her food down and she just stares at it, then she looks at you like "What's this crap? I come to this establishment a lot. I know the owner. So what's the deal here?" She may take a few bites, or she may just walk away with her nose up in the air.

You can feel the air get chilly. The paradigm has changed. You've got to find something new that your now demonic cat from hell is willing to eat. The search is on.

And you're screwed.

Why don't cat food makers have sample size pouches of dry food so that you can figure out a new diet. (And I don't count those little pouches of "treats". Those are never the same as the regular dry food; that's why they're a 'treat') Nope, you have to buy five and ten pound bags instead. Now if your cat will just eat its own weight in a new food, *before* telling you it doesn't like it by barfing it up on the freshly cleaned living room carpet.

Or maybe you can just switch to all wet food; your choice of a seafood mix or a meat mix. (But most vets suggest a mix of both wet and dry.) Besides, those little single serve cans are cute but just figure out what they are really costing you and you'll go back to the dry food aisle. (You might as well be mincing up filet mignon for your kitty.)

I figured that switching the meaty paste stuff first was the cheapest way to go. You *can* get individual portions of different wet foods, so you don't have to commit to a whole bag of something your cat may reject with her first bite. (Hell, she may just *sniff* it and walk away.) After trying a couple different wet foods from the same manufacturer that were duly rejected, I decided that maybe all that company's stuff had a similar smell or something. So I switched to a different manufacturer, and tried a couple cans of their stuff. Nope. Krysla didn't like any of it.

So I went back to maybe it was the dry stuff that wasn't appetizing any more. I had used a different manufacturer's dry stuff before and Krysla had rejected it, so I stayed with the same company but a different dry mix. I bought the smallest bag I could find and just put about a dozen crunchies down for her to try. After a few sniffs and one taste, she walked away. I went and had a beer and watched TV for a half hour. I had to try something, but when I walked back in the kitchen, to my surprise all the crunchies were gone. The sly minx had scarffed them down when I wasn't looking.

Ok, cool. We have a winner!

So I gave her a full portion of the new stuff and walled into the next room. After a few moments, I heard the distinctive *scrunch* of crunchies meeting their doom. With a smile on my face I went back to the TV and watched the rest of my show. Krysla came in, licked her whickers and then barfed the new food all over the throw rug. So much for the new food I thought. Then I remembered that when switching a cat to a new dry food, you should mix some of the new in with the old, gradually increasing the new food until that's all she's eating.

So I tried that. It worked. I started giving her the old wet food with the new dry and everything disappeared from the bowl. (And it didn't reappear anywhere else.)

Again, I am not a vet, but this worked for me. If your cat starts vomiting consistently, call your vet, it may be something other than the food.

All fluffed up.

There are two basic types of fluffing up.
1. It's 20 below zero outside and I've been waiting on the porch for hours, and:
2. Don't *DO* that!

Remember the episode of *Seinfeld* where George Castanza is tired of being cold in the winter and he gets a "puffy" coat? You know the kind of coat; it's overfilled with stuffing like your Uncle Stan's stomach on Thanksgiving. It's packed so tight that it's just short of exploding. You can barely move in it. I imagine every little kid in a Northern state knows what it's like to be squeezed into that kind of a winter snow suit. (And it takes so long to get into it; it's usually true that by then you need to go pee.)

In a cat's case, they can fluff up like that all on their own.

I won't bore you with the science behind a cat's ability to do this. Dogs can do it too, but it just doesn't look the same when they do it. Maybe it's having heavier fur or something, I don't really know. But when a cat fluffs up, you know it. (I know, I know. Most animals with fur coats can do this. Humans can do it too, but we don't have the fur coats anymore. It's called gooseflesh when it happens to you and me.)

And the phrase of "Being all fluffed up." came from a girl at a party. It was some time in the dead of winter. Wind howling outside. Snow flakes so big you could get a concussion if one hit you in the head. She saw Krysla come in from outside and she walked over to the cat and said, "Ah, the kitty's all fluffed up. I'll just have to deflate some of that hair." The girl used one hand on each side of Krysla and stroked her in one big stroke pulling back from head to tail. You could almost hear all the air escaping from the hair in a "whoosh." And the next sound you heard was Krysla giving a pissed off meow and puffing right back up again. Krysla did not like her fluff being forcibly deflated. She would do it in her own sweet time thank you very much.

And that's the second reason for getting fluffed up.

It's one of the most unforgettable images of a cat; the hunch backed, hair standing straight up silhouette of a black cat on Halloween decorations. The cat's tail is sticking out all bristly, looking more like a saw fish's bill that the hair on a cat. It looks like you could take it and comb your own hair with it. That's what I mean by a "Don't *do* that!" moment in a cat's life. It's sort of like when a guy feels that first touch of the proctologist's gloved finger during the prostate exam. (And never once has one of those doctors bought me a nice meal first.)

When you suddenly surprise a cat; you get instant fluff.

Josey and Krysla both looked like they doubled in size when they fluffed up, and they were short hairs. Rhianna was a long hair and she basically turned into a round ball of fur with two eyes and claws. Oh, yeah. That's the other part of a "Don't do that!" fluffing. Watch out for the claws. I think there is a direct connection in the cat's brain that when the fur stands on end, the claws pop out. You can quickly (*very* quickly) end up looking like a ninja's practice dummy.

I miss you. (So I left a present in your slipper.)

When I moved from Ohio to Arizona I had to leave Krysla behind with a friend. That was hard, but I didn't think she would be able to handle the change in climate or the fact that I would be bouncing around for a while until I had my own place again. As it turned out it was several years before I had my own apartment, and that was in California. I had to come back to Ohio a couple times and each trip it was hard to leave her behind again. And I'm sure it was hard on her too.

When I was first able to make a trip back to Ohio, I was looking forward to seeing Krysla. (And seeing my best friend too.) She came running as soon as she heard my voice, so obviously she remembered me. She was all over me, rubbing her face against me and just so happy to see me. She curled up in bed with me that night like I had never been gone. Then in about a week, I had to leave and go back to what was now my new home. It was so hard to leave her behind, but the building where I lived had a "no cats" rule. How do you leave a "Sorry, I have to go." note for a pet?

It was over a year before I could make another return visit.

This time, she still remembered me, but she was hesitant. She stopped a few feet away and just looked at me. I could almost feel the question of "Why did you leave me again?" in her eyes. After dinner, we made up and were buddies like old times. Well, not quite like old times. I swear she knew I was going to leave again. It almost hurt to leave. Little did I know that it would be over a decade before I made it back again. Just before I was to return, I called my friend to clear up some details of the trip. I asked about Krysla and that's when he told me that she had died about a month earlier. He hadn't told me then because he knew I was going to be upset that I wasn't there when she passed.

When I got back to Ohio and we were talking about Krysla, he said that she used to go in my bedroom after I left and meow for me, trying to find out where I was. She would sleep in my bed for a few days, then she would return, dejected, to my friend's bed. That's one way a pet deals with abandonment issues. (Because in Krysla's mind; I had abandoned her.)

Josey was different.

When Allison went away to college, it was the first time that she and Josey had been apart for any length of time. Josey reacted in the same way as Krysla in a couple of aspects. She meowed for her, and slept in her bed. Then she started something new. Josey started peeing on Allison's bed. And in her shoes.

I'm sure Josey was mad and upset that she had been abandoned; after all, we think she was an undomesticated kitten and she might have a memory of suddenly no longer having a mother around. Allison, in this case, was Josey's mother substitute. (Just as I am today.) But can a cat actually feel anger and being upset? I don't know for certain, but I don't think their emotional makeup is that complex. More than likely, Josey was acting out and trying to cover up Allison's scent with her own. And Allison's bed and shoes would be places where her scent was concentrated.

My friends here had warned me that Josey had left "presents" in Allison's room after she went to college. I said to not worry about it; I had never had a problem like that with a cat.

I am still crossing my fingers every time I go to Ohio to see family and friends in the hope that Josey won't prove me different. (And my mattress pad has a plastic backing just in case I'm wrong.)

Just like a teenager. (I won't be home tonight.)

The other night Josey decided (on her own, I wasn't consulted at all) that she was going to spend the night out.

Maybe she'd be staying over with cat friends. Maybe she'd play some cards. Maybe she'd have some pizza, or Chinese take out. Maybe she forgot to wear her watch and the time got away from her. That's a whole lot of "maybes". Whatever the reason, she just didn't come home. Next time I saw Allison (her first owner) I asked her about it. She said that Josey had done this before a few times and that she would just be waiting on the front steps come morning.

True enough, the next time an all-nighter happened, I realized that Allison had been right. Early the next morning, Josey *was* there, all fluffed up against the cold and ready for breakfast. She strode into the house like nothing had happened. Then while she had her crunchies, I gave her a long lecture about the importance of being in contact and letting me know if she was going to stay out for the night. Of course, it went in one ear and out the other. (Okay, when did I turn into my mother?)

Still, you have to wonder; just where does your "indoor" cat disappear to when she stays out for the night? In Josey's case, I'm just certain that she is being waylaid by a group of the neighborhood cats who lead her astray. (Damn. That's my mother again.)

Okay, okay. She has probably just gone on a "walk-about" as the Australians say. Either something got her attention enough that it distracted her into a further investigation, or she decided that she just had to get away from all the pressures at home. Now, just how much "pressure" can be put on an animal that spends sixteen hours a day sleeping, I'm not sure. I would think that that much sleeping would give you a relatively relaxed attitude towards virtually everything. (*If*, you could be woken up long enough to be asked about it.)

Could a cat just need to get away from her humans for a day?

Well, think about it. You always hear people griping about how they "just need to get away from this crap for a while." Do our cats view us as the "crap" in their lives that they need to get away from? Yes, we give the little beasties a roof over their heads, food, companionship, and in most cases, more love than we probably give our kids. Is that *too* much? Are we smothering them and making life too easy for them so they feel a need to have a night out and visit their wild side? (Or maybe I am over analyzing this and I should up my visits to the shrink to twice a week.)

Of course when we're talking about getting away from something, we are usually talking about our jobs or something at our job that is bugging us. Last time I checked, cats don't have jobs. (Except for farm cats that still live in the barns.)

Well, wait a minute. Maybe cats do have a job. Maybe *we* are their job. Dogs were domesticated by man to work for him. Cats domesticated man so that they had something to do other than eat, sleep and reproduce. Something so they could feel fulfillment in their lives.

Yeah, that's it. We are our cat's job.

Man. I wouldn't wish that job on anyone.

Do you see something there? (Because I don't.)

I swear there are times when Krysla would see stuff in our house that I couldn't see.

There were rumors that the house was haunted before I bought it, and frankly, that didn't deter me at all from buying it. There were many houses in my hometown that were said to be haunted. Supposedly we had a lot of Civil War ghosts in the area. (This didn't make sense because there was only maybe one Civil War battle that had been fought in the area and it was minor.) However, the Underground Railroad that moved runaway slaves north to Canada did pass thru my hometown. Whatever, just to make sure, I visited a local lady that read palms and such things and asked her what to do if my house *was* haunted. She told me to just announce to the spirit that I would respect its right to be there if it would respect mine. I figured what the hell and did it; never had any problems after that. (Of course, I hadn't actually had any to begin with either.)

It was interesting that, though I felt okay in the house, I swear Krysla was chasing ghosts at times. Maybe she was just playing cat games that only they understand; like a game of tag with an imaginary friend. I'd had an imaginary friend when I was little, so who's to say my cat couldn't have one? Cats are intelligent animals after all, and part of intelligence is being able to conceive of imaginary things.

I was always curious about what Krysla was chasing when she was running around the house. I had thought it was probably just some bug that had caught her attention by flying thru a sunbeam. After all, I had seen her chasing various insects at different times. (Such a killer instinct when she was up against the horrible flying menace of a Lady Bug.) However, there were times when she didn't seem to be just playing. So, was there something there that I couldn't see?

There was a story that I had read once, that said there were "monsters" or "supernatural beings" (or maybe it was "dust bunnies") that existed in another dimension, but occasionally you could see them in the corner of your eye. That's why you would catch these fleeting images of *something* that you just couldn't quite see. (An interesting idea that someone will probably get a government grant to study.) Maybe the corner of Krysla's eye was bigger than mine and she could "see" these beings that I couldn't.

And maybe it was just a Lady Bug.

You're driving me nuts (And it's a really short drive.)

She's doing stuff that drives you nuts.

There's the "I want out, I want in" maneuver where she makes a commotion until you let her out. She's back inside in ten minutes. Takes the last leftover bite of her dinner, and then she's rubbing up against the door and meowing to get out. She's not in heat and you saw her peeing in the garden. What the hell is wrong with your cat?

I vote for – she's just crazy.

But alas, she's just being a cat.

Both Josey and Krysla did this, and with both cats I finally figured out the answer. Both of these kitties were just overheating a little because there was a new Tom in the neighborhood. And like teenagers when a new boy transfers into their school, they have got to check the new guy out. Josey is running inside to change into a new outfit because the potential Tom Terrific has already seen her in this fur coat. Once inside, Josey realizes that she only has one outfit. That's when she decides that she just has to go back out and show it off in a different way. "Maybe I'll show him from the top of the deck rail. Yeah, the light is good up there. It will show off the highlights in my fur." So she's back outside doing a catwalk back and forth on the deck rail while Tom is nonchalantly grooming his paws down below.

Josey doesn't notice her buddy, (the tabby next door that looks like her) is watching from a window in his house. He just can't wait till he can get outside and introduce himself to the new guy. He's flexing one paw, then the other in anticipation. Tabby outweighs New Tom by a good five pounds, which in cat terms means Tabby is a sumo compared to New Tom's middle weight. It's gonna get ugly in the backyard tonight. But that's just cats being cats.

Then there is the sniffing and pawing at the end table.

Your cat is constantly going back to the end table (it's really a small cabinet, but you call it a table) by the sofa. She sniffs it. She rubs up against it. She gets her chin right down on the carpet and looks under it. Then she loses interest and just wanders off like it's no big deal. Later, she's back at it again. Sniff. Rub. She sticks one paw under it as far as it will go. Her tail is moving in big sweeps on the carpet. Finally, you can't stand it any more. You ask your husband if he thinks there could be a pest, a mouse or something, under the table. He grunts and mumbles something. You had hoped he would take the hint and look, but the sports page has wrapped around his brain and won't let go. You move the lamp from the table and with some effort push the table aside (it's full of books you plan on reading some day), all the while expecting something to scurry away from underneath it.

Nope, dead center where your cat couldn't get to it is her favorite toy. It must have rolled there when she was playing with it. You pick it up and shake it. The noise activates a flurry of scrambling feet from the other room as your cat rushes into this room. She comes right up to the toy and sniffs it. You shake it and toss it aside for her to play with it. She runs over, bats it a couple times with her paws. She sniffs it one last time and then tail in the air, she walks away, leaving the toy on the floor.

Now wasn't that worth it?

Hell no. At least she could have played with it for a while, or taken it with her like it meant something.

Again, that's a cat being a cat. If you try to figure out why they are doing something, it will just drive you crazy. Unless there is some serious insanity going on that you think you should call the vet and ask him about, (like hissing, spitting or throwing up) I just let her be a cat.

But do keep an eye out for abnormal behavior. And play with her. I have found that a lot of Josey acting up is just to get my attention. I play with her and she settles down. She tends to forget that when I am busy and don't have time for her, well , that's just a human being a human.

You realize that I can't see thru you?

It has happened to all of us.

You are sitting watching the TV, or working at the computer, or even reading a magazine and your cat comes over and immediately crawls into your lap or sits on your keyboard or whatever it takes to get your attention.

At least I think Josey wants my attention. When I'm watching TV or reading and she crawls in my lap, sometimes she will look at me and I won't have the slightest idea of what she wants. So I just look back at her. She blinks first. That's Checkmate; I win. But other times she will rub her face against my arm, and then settle in for a nap like I'm just this big warm (and soft) pillow to her. Another time, she will appear, settle in and when I don't do anything, she will actually try to push her head under my hand. This is our universal signal that means she wants me to rub her head. (And maybe a little cheek rubbing too.) So the last one is definitely "I want attention", but I think the others may just be "I want to socialize".

But what about when she appears, settles in, tries to find a comfortable position but doesn't, so leaves? What's that all about? "Sorry, you were too lumpy. Just what did you have for dinner?" Was that attention, socialize, bad after dinner date? You'll never know, because like all cats, Josey feels that she doesn't have to explain her actions. ("That's part of the mystique" my ass, little lady, I want some answers.)

Ah, but what has to be the all time infuriating maneuver is the walking in front of the computer screen and just sitting there like a sphinx.

With Krysla I didn't have to worry about this. It was in the Dark Ages and I was writing on a Smith-Corona portable typewriter. I don't even think home computers had been invented yet. (Computers yes, but not a desk top unit for word processing.) Krysla would come up beside the typewriter and try to catch the carriage arms as they headed towards the paper. When that had pissed her off enough, she would just curl up there and give the machine the evil eye. Or she would move over into my lap and give me the evil eye.

Josey however is around during this Enlightened Age of home computing. (Even though tablets are now taking over from desk tops.) Since there is desk space between the flat screen and the keyboard, she has (like all cats would) decided that that is a space that she is allowed to fill. And fill it she does. She will walk up and just stop in front of the screen. Then she will sit down and either stare at me with that "What?" look on her face, or just close her eyes and do the sphinx imitation. Or what really gets my fur up, is when she just curls up in a ball and goes to sleep. (And I hate it when she turns her head upside down when she's sleeping. It's like a "Nah, nah a nah, nah.")

This cannot in any way be considered a cry for attention. You know how many games of solitaire she's interrupted? (And some serious work too.)

So, what's she trying to tell me? That she's part of the family, or that she can just become part of the room and not be noticed? (That would be very Zen of her; I am part of the room. Om-m-m-m.) She can almost pull it off except when one of her paws "accidentally" falls over the edge of the desk and strikes a key. (I saw that, Grasshopper.)

Attention hog or sphinx? It's her choice and I doubt if I will ever understand either one.

What did you do to my waterbed?

When I lived in the house in Ohio, I had a king size water bed.

Krysla loved it. She would run circles on it (occasionally missing a turn and sliding off onto the floor) especially when I had the satin comforter on it. (It was a gift.) It had a bookcase headboard (yes, this was the early Seventies) where she could curl up with her favorite book or watch the TV. The bookcase openings were like her own little kitty caves. She used to like the opening above my head, but that was where I kept my alarm clock. When the alarm went off, she would puff up until she barely fit in the space and hiss at it until I shut it off. Surprisingly, she didn't just run away from it. I think she had decided it was her kitty cave and no damn human noise box was going to make her give it up. (She had spent a lot of time decorating it.) But one day she had moved a couple openings over to another space. I think she moved because I kept smacking her when I was going for the snooze button.

The bed had four big king size pillows. One was always kept on a chair beside the bed for any guests that might have stayed overnight. I had two pillows. And Krysla had her pillow. As she got older, I think the hard surface of the headboard was a little too much for her and she moved to the extra pillow on the bed. Unlike Josey who likes to sleep at the end of the bed on a towel, Krysla liked a big soft pillow. She would walk up on it and pawdle it until she found just the right spot for her head. After tucking her front paws under her breast, she would give one last wiggle to settle herself in and then she'd go to sleep. Sometimes I would wake up and turn towards her and see her cute little face, and other times I would be greeted by her big furry butt.

Because I was living in Ohio at the time, I had put a heating pad under the water bladder to keep the bed warm. Even in the summer if the water inside got too cold (just a few degrees lower than body temperature) it would just suck the heat out of your body. Instead of waking up rested, you would arise slowly and with lots of stiff muscles. It took almost a day for the water to get up to temperature, so I kept the covers on it even in the summer.

Once, I was going to be gone all weekend and I stripped the bed of sheets, mattress pad and everything else so I could launder all the covers. Plus, every couple of years, I would strip off the bed and wipe down the bladder top and sides where I could reach with disinfectant. The bed would start to get funky after a while if you didn't do this. Having gotten all this laundry done and the bed wiped down, I went away for my weekend.

Coming home, I reached under the comforter that was back on the bed. Good. My roommate had actually done what I wanted and turned the water heater back on the day before and put the comforter on the bed to trap the heat. (Otherwise you were just heating the room.) I went and gathered up my sheets etc and got ready to make up the bed. I wanted a quick nap before dinner. Krysla had wandered into the room after making herself obnoxious upon my return. I pulled the comforter off onto the floor. Sitting on the edge of the bed frame, I dropped my body back onto the water bladder.

And as I lay there on the warm surface, I realized I was getting **wet!**

Scrambling off the bed, I reached around to feel my back. Yep, I was wet. Damn it. I had only had one leak in all the years I had had the bed. Krysla had jumped down on the bed and was taking a step, then shaking water off her paw, then another step and shake the water. I pushed on the bed and tiny streams of water squirted from the bed. What the hell?! I pushed down hard on the bed and more water squirted up from dozens of tiny holes. As I was trying to figure this out, Krysla took off across the bed. She was chasing something that I couldn't see. She stopped with both paws together like she had trapped something. I eased my hands under her and lifted her up. To my surprise, I saw a two inch wide air bubble moving in the bladder.

Krysla squirmed out of my grasp and began chasing the air bubble all over the bed. When she thought she had it trapped, I saw her claws were out. It was a WTF moment. I pushed on the bladder and realized that the water squirted up out of a tiny arc of holes. I was certain that if I could hold her long enough I would find that those holes matched the claws on Krysla's front paws.

While I was gone and the bed was uncovered for two days, Krysla had had a wonderful time chasing the bubble on the bed. Every once in a while she would slap her paw down hard enough that her claws would penetrate the water bladder. (Over the years the bladder had stretched and thinned with age.) I was looking at a weekend's worth of fun for my cat.

I called my friend at the local head shop where I had bought the bed and told him I needed every patch kit he had for a waterbed. It took me most of the evening to patch all the holes. The whole time, Krysla watched from the pillow on the chair with that Mona Lisa smile on her face.

You like to watch. (Why?)

Krysla was a voyeur.

Talking with friends, I have found that many cats (and dogs) like to watch humans being animals. I'm not quite sure of what the attraction is. We must look quite disgusting to them in our hairlessness.

Krysla was the first cat that was always around me when I was ... dating, but she wasn't the first cat that I found watching me. I had just turned nineteen and had met someone at a bar. After a few drinks, we ended up at her trailer. It was only afterwards that I noticed the cat lazily lying on her side, watching us from her perch on the girl's dresser across the room. Not quite a sphinx, she started washing her paws as we were having a smoke afterwards. When I asked about the cat, the girl said her name and said she was always watching. It had creeped the girl out a little at first she said, and then she just ended up ignoring the cat. I couldn't. I made some excuse and left.

Now why would this have made a normal horny nineteen-year-old male leave what would have been an extended night of "dating"? It was just a cat. I didn't know why at the time, but it just felt weird having a cat watch. (Not that I would prefer any other animal or human to watch instead.) Months later, a similar episode occurred: only it was a dog this time. When we were done, I sensed something behind me. I turned and saw a large black lab, his chin resting on the side of the bed, looking at me. He did that thing dogs do where he lifted one eyebrow, then the other. Normally that would have been funny to me, but this time I felt he was being judgmental. It was like he was saying, "That was okay, but nothing special." (OK, maybe it was the pot speaking.) Again, I made an earlier than needed exit.

When Krysla came into my life, I was dating an older woman who also had a calico named "Owl." It wasn't on the first night but early in that relationship I noticed Owl watching from the dresser. (That really seemed to be the preferred vantage point.) I asked this woman about Owl and she said it used to drive her husband crazy when he caught the cat in the room. She figured that was because the ex's performance hadn't been all that great and she guessed he didn't want any witnesses. She asked if I was bothered by Owl being there. I said I guess it was ok, as long as Owl couldn't use a camera. She assured me that the cat was unable to use any type of photographic equipment and we went on the have an off and on relationship for several years. Owl was usually present at the finish. When the action moved to my house, Krysla took over the voyeuristic duties from Owl. (I think they met and compared notes.)

As I said earlier, most of my friends have had similar experiences with their pets. Only one had any real qualms and that was about a parrot that had learned certain phrases that shouldn't be repeated in polite company.

So why are our pets voyeurs? What makes them want to watch?

I have never asked a vet, but I think it might be that the couple in question is probably giving off a lot of pheromones. You pump a bunch of human musk and whatever other fragrant emissions we give off into a room and you are bound to attract an animal that spends a lot of time and effort marking her territory with scents. Ok, that might explain the attraction to the scene, but what makes the kitties want to stay and watch? (Krysla started bringing a bowl of popcorn to my room when certain girls were there.)

That's the million dollar question; what makes them stay and watch? Damned if I know. Chalk it up to one more quirk of the animal kingdom.

I'm not going to worry unless Josey starts bringing friends and I hear the popcorn popping in the microwave.

The meow that probably saved my face.

It had been a long day and I was making dinner.
Nothing special.
Chicken casserole and a chopped salad.

I had the chicken pre-cooked and was mixing the vegetables with the condensed canned soup just like my mom had always done. Without thinking, I put a tempered glass casserole dish on the range top, then reached back and turned the burner on to start the water boiling for the noodles.

Having fed Josey earlier, I had watched her saunter her way towards the front door. (She needed her après meal pee.) She stopped halfway down the hall to give herself a quick grooming on her muzzle and whiskers. (Must look good for the boys outside.) I was distracted by a noise in the kitchen; a high pitched noise of some sort. Then Josey meowed like she needed immediate attention and I walked out of the kitchen to go let Josey out. (She could be a pain if she couldn't go out on her schedule, not mine.)

I was just a couple steps out of the kitchen, when the high pitched noise increased and suddenly there was an explosion behind me!

I felt something hit my back. There was noise like chunks of something heavy hitting the walls in the kitchen. I couldn't figure it out.

Turning around, I saw big pieces of thick glass and shards of broken glass all over the floor. I had placed a tempered glass dish on a burner on the stovetop and instead of turning on the burner under the water pot; I had turned the burner on high under the empty dish. Now, tempered glass is a tough material. I had spent 20+ years in commercial kitchens as a cook and chef, and had never seen a dish like that explode, (break yes, but explode - no) but that's what had happened to this one. It is not designed for this kind of abuse. Pieces had gone everywhere in the kitchen.

It was only then that I realized that if Josey hadn't meowed to get my attention when she did, and get me out of the kitchen at exactly that moment, I would probably have had a face full of glass right then. I picked up a two inch shard that looked like a mini javelin and wondered what that would have done to my rugged good looks. There were big chunks of the dish melting their way into soft rubber mats we had on the floor in front of the oven and the sink. Glass was everywhere. On the floor, the counters, the range top. I threw away the food that was exposed because I wasn't going to take a chance that someone might eat glass.

I yelled for everyone to stay out of the kitchen and started picking up pieces. Both my roommates are nurses and one came to see what had happened and then to help clean up. He said I was lucky to have not been in the kitchen when it happened or we would be on our way to the hospital in an ambulance. ("If I was even alive" a little voice in my head told me.)

Later that evening, I was lying in bed with Josey curled up in her normal ready for bedtime spot (in my armpit) while I scratched her head and stroked the top of her nose (which she particularly liked).

I *knew* that there was no way that she *knew* that that dish was going to explode. But I also knew that if she hadn't meowed to get my attention and get me out of that room, I might not be alive to write this book.

And that's the most important reason for me to write this.

To say thanks.

Saying goodbye to an old friend.

As I am writing this, my nephew has to decide about putting his cat Tigger to sleep.

I remember Tigger as this little gray and white tiger striped streak of energy that practically bounced off the walls, hence his name. But that was 23 years ago. That is *ancient* for a cat. He's slowed down to a crawl now. Not the young cat that seemed like he could leap from the floor to a cross timber in the wooden cabin my nephew was renting when I first met Tigger. Now he needs help to get up on the couch.

This is usually a horrible decision for any pet owner, whether you have a cat or dog or cockatiel or even the guy with the Komodo dragon.

Pets are *family*. Hell, most people like their pets *better* than their family.

It is especially hard to have to make the conscious decision to put a pet down. If your little beastie is taken away suddenly via accident, health problem or whatever, that is one thing. It is a whole different thing when you have to decide for your little guy. I was lucky with Krysla. She was hit by a car while she was chasing a squirrel across the street. That may not sound lucky, but she was old, her health was starting to fail and she was doing something that she enjoyed at the end.

Though you never want to see your pet go, sometimes it is best for your pet for you to make that decision. He goes to sleep while you are holding him, and then you can honor him properly by giving him a decent burial. That is much better than being greedy and wanting to keep him around for you even though he's in a lot of pain etc.

He's been a good friend and companion. It's time to let him go.

You will always have the memories.

In Memoriam.

This is a partial list of the cats that I have mentioned in this book and that I have been honored to know:

My cats –

     Krysla   -   1973 to 1990, aged 17

     Smoker -   1983 to 1991, aged 8

My sister Connie's cats –

     Sneakers –   1985 to 2005, aged 20

     Mr. Stubbs (Stubby) –   1993 to 2007, aged 14

My nephew Stuart's cat –

     Tigger -   1990 to 2013, aged 23

Jim and Inez's cats –

     Valentine's Day (V.D.) –   1993 to 2008, aged 15

     Nightmare (Bubba Kitty) -   1991 to 2012, aged 21

May they all be happily playing with a big ball of yarn somewhere nice.

About the author.

Lindsay N. Pendragon was born and raised in North Central Ohio. He grew up in Wooster and attended Akron University. After working in the family appliance business, which he expanded into records and stereos (this was the 1970's), he moved west and lived in Arizona and California until 1992. Out there, he worked, usually as a cook and/or a baker, in the kitchens of various restaurants in Ventura and Oxnard. He also spent a couple of years working in the landscape design business as a draftsman and estimator. Once he had moved back to Ohio in 1992, he worked in and supervised warehouses.

He became partially disabled and has semi-retired to Jamestown in North Carolina just outside of Greensboro in 2012 where he now lives with Josey the cat and three friends. He is currently working on another book.

You can contact the author at: **Lindsays.cat.book@gmail.com**

The author is donating 5% of his royalties from this book to various Humane Societies and Animal Shelters.

Watch for an illustrated version of this book in 2014.

Printed in Great Britain
by Amazon.co.uk, Ltd.,
Marston Gate.